P9-CCJ-000

UNPARDONABLE CRIMES:
THE LEGACY OF
FIDEL CASTRO

Untold Tales of the Cuban Revolution

by

Celestino Heres

Author of The Reluctant Revolutionary, © 2003

Order this book online at www.trafford.com
or email orders@trafford.com

Most Trafford titles are also available at major online book retailers.

© Copyright 2003, 2010 Celestino Heres.
All rights reserved. No part of this publication may be reproduced, stored in a retrieval
system, or transmitted, in any form or by any means, electronic, mechanical, photocopying,
recording, or otherwise, without the written prior permission of the author.

The views expressed in this work are solely those of the author and do not necessarily reflect
the views of the publisher, and the publisher hereby disclaims any responsibility for them.

Edited by: Richard Anderson, Ed.D.

Printed in the United States of America.

ISBN: 978-1-4269-4559-5 (sc)
ISBN: 978-1-4269-4560-1 (hc)
ISBN: 978-1-4269-4561-8 (e)

Library of Congress Control Number: 2010914947

*Our mission is to efficiently provide the world's finest, most comprehensive book publishing
service, enabling every author to experience success. To find out how to publish your
book, your way, and have it available worldwide, visit us online at www.trafford.com*

Trafford rev. 10/29/2010

 www.trafford.com

North America & international
toll-free: 1 888 232 4444 (USA & Canada)
phone: 250 383 6864 ♦ fax: 812 355 4082

All of the stories in this book, although written as fiction, are based on real events narrated to me by my family and friends. The first story in this collection, "From Buchenwald to Connecticut," was told to me by my father-in-law, Raul, a jewelry manufacturer in Cuba. "Bitter Victory," the second story, was told to me by my two dearest friends who suffered imprisonment in Castro's gulag. The third story, "Bullet Holes in the Marble Wall," was related to me by my father, a native of Spain, who came from the same province as the Lescano family, the main characters in the story.

As for the rest of the tales, they were born from the myriad conversations I've had with many Cuban friends during the forty plus years of vacations in Miami, a city of a million stories and the temporary "home" of thousands of disenfranchised Cuban refugees.

Everyone has a story to tell, and oftentimes there is a story behind a story. I was afraid that many of the events that actually occurred in Cuba prior to, during, and after the Revolution would never be made public. As is often the case with stories of war, many are never told and go to the graves with the men and women who lived them, like footprints in the sand after the rising of the tide. In this collection you will find a common thread: the struggle of Cubans to survive under the cruel oppression of Fidel Castro and Fidel's betrayal of his own people. Betrayal? Yes!

Cubans had envisioned a glorious democratic revolution.

Dedication

I dedicate this book to my grandchildren Krista, Ever and Katarina. Also to my fellow cubans , both living or deceased, who suffered directly or indirectly at the hands of Fidel Castro and his nefarious regime.

Acknowledgements

My deepest gratitude to my friends in Moscow, Russia; Montreal, Canada and Miami, Florida. They know who they are. My thanks also goes to my friend and editor Richard Anderson who worked through many versions of these tales to make them worthy of publication. To both, my daughter Elsa Marie and my son-in-law John Hungaski, Jr., for designing the front cover of the book.

A Note to the Reader

In writing these tales I have tried to be as factual as possible, but this should be considered a work of fiction. I have taken artistic license with several characters, time frames, and locals. I would ask the reader to overlook these minor rearrangements and appreciate the panoply of human dreams and struggles, their tragedies and their triumphs.

Table of Contents

From Buchenwald to Connecticut

"In the truest sense, freedom cannot be bestowed; it must be achieved."

Franklin D. Roosevelt

In the summer of 1969, Saul and Hannah Yelin finally came to the conclusion that they must escape from communist Cuba. Years prior, Saul's mother, Elena, one of the survivors of the Buchenwald Nazi concentration camp, had migrated to Cuba, leaving behind Abraham Yelin, her husband, in a pile of ashes at Auschwitz. Elena and her son Saul entered Cuba when he was only fifteen years old. In Cuba, Saul, a thin, dark haired, shy boy, grew up and married Hannah, his high school sweetheart. They had two beautiful daughters, but decided that the best place for Yakira and Luisa was not in Cuba. Even though almost nine years had elapsed since Saul and Hannah had sent the girls to grow up and study in Greenwich, Connecticut, the couple remained behind in Cuba for one very good reason.

Even in the darkest moments of the early Cuban Revolution, Saul and Hannah never thought of leaving the island they loved so much. The main reason their daughters were sent to the United States was to protect them from communist indoctrination. But now, with Saul's beloved mother deceased and his business taken over by the communists, there was nothing left for him in Cuba. It broke his heart to see all of his jewelry making machinery, presses, lathes, welding equipment, etc., removed from his factory by Castro's soldiers. Saul especially valued the state of the art machinery press he had bought in Trenton, New Jersey, during the summer of 1958 for $10,000, a very large sum in those days. It was a specially designed press he intended to use to enter a new, lucrative market in Cuba: the production of high school and college graduation rings. Purchasing a graduation ring with your school's insignia became an established fad; not only was it a piece of jewelry to wear daily, but a ring was also something that was exchanged between high school sweethearts. Girls would proudly wear their boyfriend's ring on a necklace or on one of their fingers. Unfortunately, Saul never had a chance to use the machine.

When soldiers arrived at the doorstep of his jewelry store one overcast spring morning, he escorted them straight to the safe he kept in the back room of the shop. He did this to satisfy the soldiers' greed; he had heard stories of these disgruntled, poorly paid soldiers who now had access to private homes and businesses. They could take whatever they wanted as long as they bribed their superiors. If they did not find something of value, they would've arrested Saul and who knows what else they would have done if money or gold had not been there to appease them. They expected to find more than the few American hundred dollar bills and damaged gold coins and chains he had in the safe. Castro's soldiers removed all of Saul's business machinery and whatever else they wanted. Everything he had worked so hard for was taken by the communists: his capital, which he lost when the Cuban currency changed; his rental apartment properties, which had taken him years to acquire; and now his jewelry business. Everything was now the property of the state.

The next morning, the Yelins made the heart wrenching decision to leave their beloved Cuba. Saul wrote a letter to his daughters in Greenwich, CT, and sent it through friends who were leaving Cuba permanently to live in the United States. He asked his daughters to make the necessary arrangements to obtain visas for their mother and himself to immigrate to the States. When the Cuban government learned of Saul and Hannah's desire to leave the country, the militia showed up again, this time at the doorstep of their home. Their six-room house, located in the beautiful Miramar district, was in one of the most desirable locations in Havana due to its proximity to the water, beautifully landscaped gardens, and the concomitant high property values that a home with an ocean view will bring. Soldiers brusquely entered their home and made a meticulous inventory of all of their personal belongings, from the blender to the sewing machine, from the furniture to the blankets and sheets; everything was carefully itemized and inventoried for now it was no longer Saul and Hannah's; it was the legal property of the state. It would only be a matter of time before their house would become someone else's, a gift for a politically connected family loyal to Fidel Castro. Soon, Saul and Yelin would be on the street.

After losing his business and his home, Saul was ordered to join a forced labor team which was assigned to clear fields and plant coffee on the outskirts of Havana. A truck would arrive early at 6:00 AM and pick up the workers at a designated location. They were drafted as forced laborers and nicknamed "gusanos" (worms) because they had applied for exit visas and were perceived as traitors to the communist regime.

At least Saul was a fairly young man; he could endure the verbal, physical, and emotional abuses the field workers were forced to endure by the military bosses. The inadequate diet and corporal punishment that the older forced laborers were also subjected to broke his heart. The brutality of the militia brought back memories of the beatings and torture suffered in the concentration camps of Nazi Germany as related to him by his mother, Elena, before she died. Luckily, their travel permits had not been permanently rescinded. Three weeks before they had to either leave the country or lose their travel permits, Saul thought it was time to play, what he deeply believed, was his winning hand. Encouraged by his mother before she became terminally ill, he had hidden some of his most valuable gold coins and his best quality diamonds and platinum jewelry inside an old iron pipe that he kept buried in the basement of his home. Before Hannah and he were forced to vacate their house, Saul unearthed the pipe and took it with him wrapped in an old blanket. In a way, the contents of the pipe had become their insurance policy. Now, the question was how to get the jewels and coins past airport security and out of Cuba?

As a result of his friendship with an Italian jeweler who owned a small shop in Havana, Saul had been able to obtain an appointment to meet with the Italian Ambassador. During the previous year Saul was commissioned to set some diamonds in a platinum bracelet that the Ambassador had purchased for his wife and, as a result, Saul developed a cordial relationship with the Italian couple. Based on this casual business relationship, Saul called the Ambassador and invited him to lunch. The Ambassador agreed, a date was set, and, on the pretense of showing the Ambassador some of the beautiful Cuban countryside, Saul picked up the Ambassador at the Embassy and drove him to a quiet little restaurant seven miles outside Havana.

The restaurant was small, but the food was good and the vista of the hills very relaxing. After finishing their lunch and enjoying coffee and cigars, Saul asked the Ambassador for a special favor: to help him send a small package containing personal items out of Cuba through diplomatic channels. The Ambassador remained silent for what felt like minutes; he then looked Saul straight into his eyes and said, "I know what an honest, hard-working, decent man you are and the tragic story of your family in Nazi Germany and now here in Cuba. I would be glad to send this package of which you speak to your daughters in the United States via Rome in a diplomatic pouch, but the only way that I can do this is for you to deliver the package directly into my hands inside the Italian Embassy. The land on which the Embassy stands, as you know, is considered Italian soil. I have received orders from my government not to get involved with any people outside the Embassy walls, but if you can figure out a way to get your package into the Embassy I can take it from there." Saul thanked the Italian Ambassador, returned home, and continued to work on his plan for he and his wife to escape Cuba with more than just their lives.

That night, when Saul told Hannah about his plan to ship their valuables out of Cuba by way of the Italian Embassy, she reminded him that he had only two weeks left before their travel permits expired. No one knew of his plan except Hannah, and Saul knew that several of his friends had been caught trying to smuggle cash out of the island and were now in jail. He also knew the old saying, "Once you tell someone a secret, it is no longer one." The trouble with the communists was you had no way to tell them apart. You might think that you were sharing a secret with one you believed was a close friend, but you might also be sharing the secret with a communist sympathizer. On the first day available, Saul began to casually visit the area around the Embassy to reconnoiter: to note how many guards, where they were stationed, and to come up with a plan to gain access to the property.

On one of his first visits by local bus to where the Italian Embassy was situated, Saul noticed a small café across the street, walked in, sat down, and ordered an espresso. While glancing out the café window to notice the comings and goings on the street and while musing over his coffee, his plan began to take form. He stood up, walked over to the counter, and identified himself to the manager of the café as the owner of a newly opened flower shop on the other side of the city. Saul explained that his mother-in-law lived a few blocks away from the café, and he was in the process of finding her a place to stay near their apartment near the store. In the back of his mind, Saul was planning to use a standard rose box, no bigger than a shoebox but smaller than a regular suitcase in which to secrete his jewels. This box could be reinforced to hold the weight of his valuables. The gold coins he would pack in cotton, the diamonds could be wrapped in the same paper they were in when he bought them in Antwerp, Belgium, many years ago. The platinum jewelry pieces were relatively light and wouldn't pose a problem wrapped in silk envelopes. His plan had been spontaneously conceived in a moment over a casual cup of coffee, a moment of insight on which he would gamble a great deal. Later that evening, Hannah agreed with his plan to deliver a box of red and yellow roses with a false bottom to the Ambassador' office. She helped prepare the package and, in the end, Saul felt that they had done an outstanding job creating a nondescript parcel that could pass for a common box of flowers. Like mailmen, deliverymen are ubiquitous and almost become invisible as they complete their rounds.

The next morning he was in high spirits when he arrived at the café at a little past 9:00 AM, a box of "roses" safely tucked under his arm. As he rounded the corner to enter the cafe to relax before crossing the street to enter the Embassy on the pretext of making a floral delivery, he noticed something that brought a chill to his spine: four militia soldiers, not the usual two, were standing guard outside the Embassy's wrought iron gates. Apparently, a rumor had circulated that a group of dissidents was planning to force their way into different foreign embassies to request political asylum, and the guards had been reinforced at all potential points of entry. Saul thought, "I'll never be able to make it now especially with these armed guards right outside the gates." As he sat in the café he hoped that two of the guards might leave their post; at times, the revolution was very disorganized and soldiers would temporarily abandon their posts to sneak a drink or a quick nap, but not on this occasion. The inability to carry out his carefully worked out plan went on for what felt like forever to Saul as he sat in the café. After waiting for about an hour, demoralized and depressed, he returned home by bus with his box of "roses."

He would go back to the café three more times, and, on each trip, soldiers, sometimes three or four, would be guarding the Embassy entrance. But, luck was on his side. Early on the morning of July 20, 1969, as Saul sat at a table by the window having a roll and coffee, he heard a tremendous noise that came from down the street. He and several others from inside the café ran out toward the noise and saw two black sedans that had collided. From his vantagepoint, two people had been ejected from one of the vehicles; one man was apparently dead, and the other, an injured woman, was lying on the street, screaming hysterically with blood streaming from her forehead. Moans were also heard coming from the interior of both smashed cars. Blood was starting to spread on the concrete among the shards of broken glass, and cries for help were echoing through the street. Suddenly, more people began running toward the accident, and, as Saul turned his head, he saw all four of the Embassy guards running down the street toward the accident scene. This was his chance.

With no hesitation, Saul slowly walked over to the unguarded Embassy entrance. Several Embassy employees had come out to the street outside of the gates to watch the scene down the street as more onlookers converged on the crash site. He walked between the employees, past the ten-foot wrought iron gates, up the white marble stairs, through the elegantly carved wooden front doors, and into the air-conditioned, beautifully appointed lobby. Saul identified himself as a personal friend of the Ambassador's wife. After being escorted to the Ambassador's private office and closing the door behind him, Saul and the Ambassador removed the contents from the bottom of the flower box and repacked them into a smaller container to be put into a diplomatic pouch. They shook hands, and Saul left the grounds before the guards returned to their post.

Two days later, Hannah and Saul Yelin departed for the United States on a flight from Havana to Miami and made their way by train to be reunited with their daughters, Yakira and Luisa, in Greenwich, Connecticut. A month and a half after their arrival in the United States, a package containing the seeds for a new beginning arrived from Rome, Italy, with the original contents intact. With the sale of these jewels, Saul and Hannah Yelin were able to open what turned out to be a successful jewelry store in Greenwich, CT.

Had she still been alive, Saul's mother, a Buchenwald survivor, would have been very proud of her son's courage and resourcefulness to elude the Cuban communists and to start a new life for his family in America. The long journey had started in Buchenwald with his mother escaping the horrors of the Nazi Holocaust and ended happily in Connecticut with Saul, Hannah, Yakira, and Luisa escaping Castro's oppression to enjoy the freedoms and opportunities of the United States.

Bitter Victory

"Under a government which imprisons any unjustly, the true place for a just man is also a prison

Henry David Thoreau

Pepe Garcia and Mongo Alonzo were both born in Havana in 1940. They lived on the same block and attended the same elementary school. When it came time to leave elementary school they applied and were admitted to Belén High School, the distinguished Jesuit school with an enrollment of 300 or so young men spanning grades 9 -12. This was the same high school that Fidel Castro had attended and graduated from in the spring of 1945.

Fidel went on to attend the University of Havana and gained a reputation as a militant. Fidel had gotten used to carrying a gun, and in April of 1948 he committed his first murder while visiting Bogota, Colombia, as a student representative from Cuba. Riots broke out in Bogota, and Fidel experienced the ending of a human life for the first time. As a teenager, Fidel had read widely, but two books had the greatest impact on him during these formative years: Adolph Hitler's Mein Kampf , which he later would use as a model for his own book, History Will Absorb Me, and Karl Marx's The Communist Manifesto. As a student at Belén, Fidel had also developed a convincing technique of concocting intricately woven and highly believable lies. Reverend Armando Llorente, a Latin instructor at Belén, had noticed Fidel's knack for rearranging the truth to suit his own needs. In the middle of one lesson when Fidel was explaining his excuse for not being prepared for the day's recitation Reverend Armando scolded Fidel right in front of his classmates and said, "Fidel, I notice that you tell many lies." Fidel just scowled. The students in the class were shocked that Reverend Armando would state this fact publicly, while all along any student at Belén who had contact with Fidel knew of his talents at manipulating the truth.

Even though Pepe and Mongo resided in Havana and were eligible to attend public high school for free, their parents decided to pay the tuition and board at Belén to provide a means of instilling the Jesuit style of discipline, a tough love approach that had proven effective for previous generations of students. On a typical school day, the students were awakened at 6:30 AM to attend Mass at 7:00, then off to breakfast, a short walk to the classroom building, lunch from 12:00 to 1:00 and, in the afternoon, to the biology, chemistry, or physics labs. On certain weekends students were eligible to leave the campus and visit their homes to see family and to hang out with their neighborhood friends, but on Sunday afternoon it was time to return to the dorm to prepare for the next week's lessons.

Their teachers were impressed by the boys' abilities to retain important facts and the speed with which they grasped complicated concepts. The Jesuits encouraged Pepe and Mongo to advance academically at speeds far beyond the rates of factual and theoretical acquisition they had seen in most of the other students they had worked with. Very early, Pepe and Mongo grasped the concepts of higher mathematics and science. However, their penchant for academics did not preclude a wholesome and balanced upbringing: both were members of the baseball team and leaders of the Belén Debate Club.

When Pepe and Mongo were fifteen years old and just freshmen at Belén, they listened as the older students quietly discussed politics late at night in their dormitory. They heard about Fidel Castro's attack on the Moncada barracks in Santiago de Cuba on July 26, 1953, a date that Castro used to name his organization, "Movement 26 of July." Their fellow students were caught up in the excitement of the political ferment in Havana and went on about Castro's opposition to Fulgencio Batista and how many students at other private schools who came from wealthy families had already aligned themselves with the movement. The dream of this revolutionary movement was to remove the dictator and replace him with a democratically elected president in a free and independent Cuba. True freedom meant a government not controlled by Washington, D.C. as had been the case with previous Cuban regimes.

In spite of these intense political times, Pepe and Mongo were more interested in playing baseball and dreaming about girls than entertaining any political opinions much less revolutionary ideas. However, their high school years passed quickly, and in 1958 they graduated with honors from Belén H.S. It was a turning point for each of them in many different ways. Pepe and Mongo, with diplomas in hand, started to become interested in Cuban politics. Although older and wiser academically, they were not sophisticated enough politically to understand the seriousness of what they were getting into.

They joined the resistance movement in Havana and began to participate in acts of sabotage. During one of their nightly excursions they were able to disrupt the transmission of electric power to the entire city of Havana. Their knowledge of basic electricity and physics told them that throwing long chains onto the power lines would create a power failure at the receiving stations. Havana was without electricity for seven hours. With the chaos that ensued, the president of University of Havana had no choice but to shut its doors. Without thinking ahead as far as the practical ramifications of their act of sabotage, Pepe and Mongo realized too late that they would now have to put their plans for higher education on hold. At most, they thought the University would be closed a year, a year that would perhaps change everything, and the school, the one critical place of any culture, would reopen. Their years of training, strengthened by the Jesuit drive to see what is not in front of you but to see the beauty in knowledge, was stopped dead in its tracks by a fellow Jesuit student named Fidel. Pepe, Mongo, and many other Cubans were happy that Batista had left Cuba and gone into exile on New Year's Day of 1959, that the revolution had ended, and that Fidel had won. Better days were ahead.

When Castro and his followers marched into Havana, Pepe and Mongo were among the excited crowd in the square. Riding in military vehicles and waving to the spectators, Fidel and his brothers with their long hair and beards, their rag tag uniforms, and the reflections of sunlight off their steel gray gun barrels, these country guerillas were the victors. Pepe and Mongo did not have long hair or long beards because they were "urban guerillas." Even though they didn't look like Castro and the other soldiers who had endured living in the mountains and camping out at night, they were proud of their participation in the revolutionary movement.

Like a number of other Cubans, only several months after the end of the fighting, Pepe and Mongo began to have second thoughts about their leader and this entire revolution thing. They learned about the executions being carried out at La Cabaña Fortress of those who Castro did not trust. Some of those executed had been guerilla fighters who had joined the revolution in its early stages. The direction of the revolution away from the establishment of a democratic government and towards a communist takeover, and the strange death of Camilo Cienfuegos, an admired Comandante in the rebel army, brought a change in attitude in many Cubans. Pepe, Mongo, and others felt betrayed and joined plots to try to recover the democratic revolution many had fought so hard to implement. Pepe and Mongo volunteered to participate in a scheme to carry weapons and ammunition to the Escambray Mountains where some like thinkers had gone to start a counter-revolution against Castro.

They borrowed Pepe's father's automobile, a Cadillac, called a "cola de pato" or "duck's tail," loaded the car with what weapons and ammunition they could obtain, and drove from Havana towards the Escambray Mountains of south central Cuba. They naively thought that by traveling at night they would avoid detection by Castro's soldiers. They had only driven eighty miles beyond Havana on the mostly dusty, dirt roads and were just inside the city limits of Colón, when their car was stopped, they were arrested, and thrown into the local jail. The following week they were tried for treason. The trial lasted only one day, and they each received a sentence of twenty-five years in prison. The judge told them they were lucky that their lives had been spared since execution was the sentence for all counterrevolutionaries. The fact that Pepe and Mongo had been involved in the sabotage of electrical power in Havana as well as their youthful innocence were the two things that kept them from being shot.

Like most Cubans who had been put into jail as well as those who had gone into exile all over the world, Pepe and Mongo did not believe that Castro's regime would last long. Luckily, their sentences were to be carried out at a prison close to Havana so their families and friends could visit them. The many months in prison slowly turned into years, and both young men became very depressed wondering if they would be able to endure such a long sentence. Physically they were both strong, but the prospect of spending some of the best years of their lives in jail was daunting to say the least. With the bad news circulated about the embarrassing failure of the Bay of Pigs invasion, President John F. Kennedy's promise to Nikita Khrushchev that the United States would never invade Cuba, the near nuclear war precipitated by the Cuban Missile Crisis, and the lack of adequate food and decent medical attention in prison, their physical and mental health began to deteriorate to the point of total despair.

Sharing the same cell with them were two other political prisoners. One, Miguel Espinosa, had been Dean of the School of Engineering at the University of Havana, the other, Alfonso Martinez, had been employed as a mathematician at a private Presbyterian high school in Cárdenas who had a Ph.D. in General Engineering. These members of the Cuban intelligentsia, the free thinking professors who had worked at Cuba's leading educational institutions, were now considered criminals, anti-socials, and threats to Castro's regime. Ironically, while Fidel hatched some of his personal, harebrained schemes, one of which was to genetically create a "super cow," teachers such as these could have been preparing college and graduate students to build the infrastructure that Cuba's future depended on in order to compete with the world's industrialized nations. As it was, these highly talented Cubans were thrown into prison because of Fidel's paranoia and insecurity which revolved around anyone he suspected possessed an intellect superior to his own.

As a way to pass the time in prison, the professors decided to teach each other in a variety of topics in the fields of engineering, mathematics, and physics. They used the walls of the cell as chalkboards, and, using shoe oil and a twig, drew the necessary diagrams, formulas, and equations. Each shared the knowledge of his own particular expertise. There were no tests or grades; the dual purpose was to keep their minds active and to share knowledge in the academic field for which each inmate had a passion. Learning was its own reward. The prison guards thought these two men were crazy as they discussed esoteric ideas that meant nothing to them. So, the guards left them alone since they bothered no one, posed no threat, and quietly passed the time writing on the prison walls what the guards thought was just "nonsense."

The two teachers asked Pepe and Mongo if they wanted to join in. During their years at Belén, Pepe and Mongo had already completed introductory physics, organic and inorganic chemistry, and mathematics through calculus and they were started them off with a review of differential equations and moved on to advanced topics in physics and math. Miraculously, this form of entertainment cured their depression, and, as year followed year, they became as knowledgeable as their professors. Of course, the lessons did not last all day, but they were all "captive audiences" of each other. Time was also spent discussing politics and what they would do when they finally were released from prison. Luckily, no member of this group of four became seriously ill from the poor diet and lack of exercise that was limited to only one hour a day in the confines of the prison yard. There was no form of heat on the nights when temperatures dropped, and the ventilation was poor during the hot, humid days. At least the prisoners all received an adequate supply of clean drinking water, and when the "school group" asked if they could be provided with books and any other reading material the guards were kind enough to smuggle in old newspapers and magazines.

During the last five years of their imprisonment another unfortunate individual joined them in their cell. As luck would have it, he was an English teacher. Even though Ediberto was Cuban born, he had studied at an American university and had lived in the United States for twelve and a half years. His English was flawless, and he brushed off his geometry and pre-calculus with Miguel, Alfonso, Pepe, or Mongo, he began to instruct his four fellow sufferers in a new discipline. It did not take very long for Pepe and Mongo to learn English and to converse with each other and to correct each other in their newly acquired language. Miguel and Alfonso had a bit more trouble learning English but were determined. Their English professor laughed at the fact that two of his new pupils were almost geniuses in other fields but in English they were like grade school children learning the alphabet. One joke that they all shared was the universal mispronunciation of the word "kitchen:" it always sounded like someone was asking for a "key chain." Another joke involved Ediberto's first year in America teaching a 9th grade algebra I class in Darien, CT. During the second day of class Ediberto wanted each student to take out an eraser from his or her pencil case or book bag. Ediberto directly translated the Spanish word for "eraser," into English and said to the group, "Would everyone please take out their rubbers?" Laughter erupted, and one shy student approached the desk and politely explained that in the United States the correct word was "eraser." Some innocent students thought of shoe coverings worn in inclement weather, while other more worldly 9th graders snickered thinking that the new teacher was asking them to take out condoms.

After an unbelievable twenty years in prison, Pepe and Mongo were unexpectedly released. A senator from Connecticut who was visiting Cuba learned of Pepe and Mongo's incarceration and intervened on their behalf. The senator promised Castro that when he returned to Washington he would work towards the removal of the United States embargo that was hurting the Cuban economy by prohibiting access to American markets. As a result of this miraculous "amnesty," Pepe Garcia, Mongo Alonzo, and ten other prisoners from other prisons were put on a plane to Miami, Florida. These men, now in their late thirties and early forties, savored their new freedom, satisfied that they had not cooperated with their jailers in spite of the many tortures and humiliations they were forced to endure during their imprisonment. Their families and friends in Miami who had been able to escape Cuba embraced and kissed them as they deplaned and celebrated them as triumphant heroes after being held as political prisoners for two decades.

One of the major culture and time shocks Pepe and Mongo experienced was their first visit to a Miami supermarket. They could not believe their eyes at the overwhelming amount of food packed on the shelves and in the frozen food coolers. Seeing this almost limitless abundance of fresh vegetables, meat, bread, etc. brought actual tears to their eyes. Such a cornucopia of readily available foodstuffs was shocking to them after enduring years of physical deprivation during their imprisonment. Their tears were also for the people in Cuba who continued to lack anything related to the kind of consumer goods that Americans took for granted.

Like all migrants to a new country, Pepe's and Mongo's next thoughts were about getting jobs, starting a social life with members of the opposite sex, and making up for all of the lost time they spent in prison. Another thought was to contact the admissions office at the University of Miami to learn what they would have to do in order to enroll in an engineering program. All sorts of questions had to be answered. Would their Cuban high school diplomas be recognized in the United States? Would time spent at the University of Havana count at all considering they had no transcripts of their work? Would they have to take an entrance exam like the SAT? Was their English adequate in order to learn complicated engineering concepts in English that they had originally learned in Spanish? As luck would have it, the Dean of the School of Engineering at the University of Miami was

Cuban-American and was very sympathetic to their predicament. He understood the dilemma confronting Pepe and Mongo. After listening to the story of their years of "perfect attendance" at their "university behind bars" as they now called it, the Dean offered a controversial suggestion: why not take engineering exams, both oral and written, with various professors of the different schools of engineering to see if they could score high enough to be granted bachelor degrees in engineering? If they could pass these undergraduate level exams based on knowledge acquired in one of Castro's prisons, they would then be able to pursue Masters and Doctoral degrees concurrently. This idea was radical but not unheard of in the history of modern academia.

It took a few months for the details to be worked out, and the two men, not boys anymore, drilled each other and read the texts recommended by the Dean and several of the professors. They thoroughly enjoyed using the books and seeing the same formulas, graphs, and equations that they had seen drawn on the walls of their cell. When they felt that they were as ready as they ever will be for their exams, they went to one of the classroom buildings and spent hour after hour solving problems, drawing diagrams, and explaining the logic behind their solutions in English. After four full day's during one week, and four half days the next, they completed their last written and oral exams, mentally spent and all written out. When the results came in three weeks later they were elated to learn that they both had passed with high grades on all the examinations. Their professors had nothing but admiration and amazement that these newly certified engineers could have learned and retained what they did under the harsh prison circumstances. In fact, both men later passed exams to become Professional Engineers and earned the coveted P.E. license.

Armed with their new credentials, Pepe and Mongo found employment with an engineering firm right in Miami. Their lives finally seemed to reach normalcy when they both were lucky to meet and eventually marry two lovely women they had known from their childhood in Cuba who had been friends of their families and were now residing in Miami.

Pepe and Mongo had both endured the same length of imprisonment and lost twenty years of their lives behind bars; but, that was then. And now? All of their happiness as successful engineers, married, and now with families, is always somehow diminished by the thought of their Cuban "brothers and sisters" who are still living in Cuba under Castro's regime. It is as if they feel a sense of guilt because they were not alone. Their hearts go out to those who to this day remain in Cuban jails, including the three teachers who taught them so well but were not lucky enough to be granted their freedom as they had. After all the suffering Pepe Garcia and Mongo Alonzo endured for twenty years and the more recent successes they have achieved, they both feel to this day that their story, although a human triumph of determination and will, was, in actuality, one of bitter victory.

Bullet Holes in the Marble Wall

"All political power comes from the barrel of a gun. The communist party must command all the guns, that way, no guns can ever be used to command the party."

Mao Tse Tung

Teofilo and Luisa Lescano arrived in the city of Colón, in Cuba, on October 27, 1939. After three years of fighting in Spain on the side of the Republic as loyal members of the Communist Party, they crossed the France-Cataluña border and ended an exhausting chapter of their lives. In the early days of the Civil War they had met Ernest Hemingway; writer Herbert L. Matthews, a correspondent for The New York Times; and George Orwell, British writer and volunteer soldier. Teofilo and Luisa like these men very much with the exception of Hemingway who they thought drank too much and was always looking after himself. The accomplishments and acts of heroism of the Lescanos were published in reports Matthews sent to The Times in New York City. Of the three, Orwell was their favorite since they knew he was the most dedicated in the cause of the Republic. Together with Teofilo and Luisa, approximately 100,000 refuges crossed the Spanish border to escape into France.

There were many and varied reasons for being part of the Spanish Civil War, but the Lescanos wanted to fight fascism, the insidious brand of fascism that brought Italy and Germany as allies to the nationalist and monarchical leader, General Francisco Franco. At that time, the Communist Party of the Soviet Union seemed to be the only group opposed to the fascists, so, logically, the Lescanos joined in and miraculously survived three years of bitter and bloody fighting against this regime.

After spending eight months in Paris, and with the financial help of friends residing in France, Luisa and Teofilo migrated to Cuba. To relocate to Cuba was logical since Spanish was the spoken language, and they had friends from Spain who had already established themselves there. When Luisa and Teofilo arrived in Havana, these friends helped to get the couple started in business.

Luisa was pregnant and wished to have their child born in a free Cuba surrounded by native born or full-blooded Spaniards who had also settled on the island. A little girl was born and was named Dolores, in honor of Dolores Ibarruri, better known by her battle name of "La Pasionaria," a popular Communist leader of the Republic.

Settling in Colón was not easy for the Lescanos. The best they could do was to acquire a job sweeping floors in a small, corner grocery store owned by a man named Alphonso. Alphonso had escaped the tragedy of the Spanish Civil War and was a very generous Spaniard who always tried to help his fellow countrymen. Unfortunately, this good Samaritan died only fourteen months after hiring the Lescanos. Fortunately for them though, he willed all of his belongings to them, including the grocery store. Teofilo turned out to have excellent business savvy, and, together with the help of Luisa and young Dolores, the little store prospered and grew. Additional money was coming in, and Teofilo, against the advice of his wife, decided to expand by purchasing the large warehouse that was attached to the back of their store. Teofilo's decision to purchase the warehouse turned out to be one of his best business decisions. He began to purchase dry goods of all kinds and, acting as a local wholesaler, sold these goods to the bodegas (grocery stores) in the district where they lived. His stock was enormous, most of the time, the piles of sugar, bean, and rice sacks covered the height of about three floors.

In order to control the rat infestations common to the dry goods business, Teofilo obtained a few Cuban, non-poisonous, boa-like snakes, called "Santa Mariás" by the locals. It was the only business in the area without a single rat to be found. Of course, there were a few incidents when those entering the warehouse without invitation got the scare of their lives upon encountering one or more of these snakes.

As the early years in the wholesale business flew by, Dolores, still an only child, grew into a beautiful teenager full of life and vitality. She was sometimes mistaken for her mother's younger sister they looked so much alike, with their long, flowing black hair; sparkling brown eyes; full lips; olive skin; and captivating, coquettish smiles. She excelled in school, and by 1958 at the age of eighteen was ready to enter the University of Havana where she planned to study medicine. While Dolores was anxiously awaiting entrance into the University, her parents were extremely concerned with the political turmoil occurring at the University and with the revolutionary talk that had Cuba in suspense.

On January 1, 1959, Batista, the military dictator of Cuba, left the island into exile, and Fidel Castro and his rebels took over the Cuban government. Teofilo thought that the University would eventually normalize and the students would be able to continue their interrupted studies. This thought of getting back to normal day to day activities brought a temporary relief to Teofilo and Luisa who, since arriving in Cuba, had distanced themselves from all political activities. They had seen enough turmoil and bloodshed in Spain, and did not want Dolores to be exposed to such horrors. That was the main reason why they had left Spain.

When Adolph Hitler and Joseph Stalin signed the non-aggression pact and occupied sections of Poland, the Lescanos had second thoughts about their membership in the Communist Party, although they never formally resigned or cancelled their original membership. They were proud of their participation in the Spanish Civil War. Their feeling was that things would blow over, the University of Havana would open up again, and normalcy would return to the island. Unfortunately, this impression lasted for only a few months. Teofilo felt that the Soviet Union was getting a foothold in Cuba, and Fidel Castro was the ideal leader to welcome them. Fidel, his brother Raul, and Ernesto "Che" Guevara, the Argentine communist, made up the troika that would drive Cuba into the most radical form of communism.

At this same time, during one of his notoriously long television appearances, Castro announced the nationalization of all private property, from the largest corporations down to the smallest private businesses. Teofilo and Luisa were quite confident that their small, inconsequential business would not be taken over by the government in spite of what was occurring around them. After all, they were still members of the Communist Party and had established an honorable record of heroic accomplishments in battle in the Spanish Civil War. The single element that the Lescanos did not count on was the fact that Comandante Osmany Cienfuegos was assigned to oversee the reorganization of property in the city of Colón. With Fidel's Castro's carte blanch, he wielded ultimate power over the city and all of its inhabitants.

Cienfuegos was well known for his cruelty and fanatical loyalty to Fidel, and, because he was not a native of Colón, Cienfuegos had no friendships with or loyalty to anyone in the town or the region. In fact, Castro intentionally assigned Cienfuegos and other leaders into unfamiliar areas of Cuba to eliminate local favoritism. Even after Comandante Cienfuegos had taken over virtually all of the private businesses in Colón, the Lescanos still felt that their own business would be spared for the reasons cited above.

Two weeks after Cienfuegos' appointment, he paid an early morning visit at the door of the Lescano's grocery store. Teofilo and Luisa had met him once before at a function when they had been in Havana on business and received him very cordially. Upon his request, they proceeded to give him a brief tour of their small but thriving business. The front room of the store looked like any other dry goods store and did not impress the Comandante; however, when he entered the warehouse which at the time was loaded to the rafters with sacks and sacks of dry goods, Teofilo and Luisa could actually see Cienfuegos' mouth watering at the sight of so much food. This was the richest storehouse in the entire province. At one point, two small "Santa Marias" slithered past him, but he was unperturbed. He was equally fascinated by the warehouse supplies and by the snakes; he must have recognized his ancestors.

The Comandante left the store with silent nods of satisfaction without making any comments about what he had seen and congratulated the couple on the thriving business that must have taken them so much hard work to accomplish. His complimentary remarks and his general demeanor made the Lescanos feel confident that their business would be safe. They were so used to dealing with honest, hard working people in the city that they did not see through his benevolent façade; they had no idea of the kind of person with whom they were dealing.

The first thing that the Comandante did after leaving the Lescano's business was to place a direct call to Fidel Castro in Havana to tell what he had seen. Cienfuegos received nothing but the warmest congratulations from Castro and was ordered to remove the entire contents of the warehouse and ship them to the supply center in Havana as soon as possible.

The next morning, Comandante Cienfuegos came to the grocery store with an order which he had written the night before demanding the immediate transferal of the keys of the warehouse to him, the representative of the Revolution. Nothing that Teofilo said to him could change his mind. Cienfuegos even wryly suggested that as "good communists" they should realize the meaning of what was happening. The benefit to the masses superceded the benefit to any individual. The Comandante became enraged when Teofilo suggested that the goods should be given to the citizens of Colón instead of sending them to the Capital. Their pleas for fairness and their invocation of their previous dedication during the Spanish Civil War fell on deaf ears. Teofilo and Luisa had no choice but to comply with Cienfuegos' request and hand over the keys to the warehouse. The soldiers who accompanied the Comandante pushed Teofilo, Luisa, and Dolores out of the way and reminded them that the grocery store was going to be "nationalized," a euphemism for "legitimized stealing" by the new government. Teofilo and Luisa realized the true meaning of communism far too late. This was not why they fought in Spain. The battle there was against Fascism, Nazism, Franco falangism, and to established a worker's paradise. But Castro's form of communism was actually destroying the paradise the workers had created on the beautiful island of Cuba.

Teofilo was in a very desperate state of mind; it seemed that all the hard work of so many years was obliterated in only a few minutes. He simply could not tolerate this gross insult to his patriotism and began to make plans for some way to either save his business by taking his case to Fidel Castro or to ensure that Cienfuegos would not get his hands on it. After all, this was nothing compared to what they had gone through during the Spanish Civil War.

After three unsuccessful attempts to meet with Fidel to plead his case, Teofilo decided that the best thing for him to do was to set fire to his own warehouse and show the Comandante and this new breed of "so-called Communists" what an old communist was capable of doing to save his honor.

At about one AM on a cloudless Friday night, he proceeded with his plan and, gathering several cans of gasoline, he poured the accelerant all over the sacks of sugar, beans, and other warehoused dry goods. He did not want to see all of this food that could help feed the people of Colón, but he had to ensure that it would not be stolen from them either. It was amazing how quickly the fire spread and how the sacks of sugar began exploding together with everything else. There was absolutely nothing anyone could do to stop the blaze; the warehouse became an inferno burning all night long and sending flames two hundred feet into the air and lighting up the sky for miles around.

The next morning, the Comandante returned to Colón and when told about the fire he became apoplectic. He ordered his men to take a truck, go to the burned warehouse, and arrest Teofilo, Luisa, and Dolores. On the personal orders of Fidel Castro himself, Cienfuego was ordered to punish these people for obvious destruction of State owned property and to do so that would teach a lesson to any others who contemplated defying Cienfuegos' authority. In considering the different types of punishment at his disposal, Comandante Cienfuegos recalled that Teofilo and Luisa had told him that there was nothing he could do to them that they had not suffered in the Spanish Civil War. However, Dolores, their daughter, had not been in Spain. So, Cienfuegos decided to punish Teofilo and Luisa by singling out Dolores.

The three Lescanos were brought from their jail cell and pushed into Cienfuegos' office. When Cienfuegos told Teofilo and Luisa that their daughter was going to suffer for her father's act of treason, they were in total shock to think that anyone could harm their innocent girl since she had had nothing to do with the arson. There was not trial, there was no legal defense; Teofilo was going to be summarily punished in one of the most brutal ways possible. At first, they thought this could not be happening, until they were brought outside of the building and saw that a firing squad of seven soldiers had been formed and was waiting outside. Dolores was placed against the wall of the old Bank of Colón across the street from police headquarters, her hands were tied behind her back, she was blindfolded, and stood there sobbing hysterically realizing that her brief life was quickly coming to and end. On orders from the Comandante who was standing at the end of the firing line, the firing squad fired their AK-47s and her body tumbled to the ground. The velocity of the bullets and the close range from which the soldiers fired was so that the bullets penetrated her slim body and six of the bullets hit the wall behind her. All of this happened so quickly that Teofilo and Luisa were beside themselves, crying and screaming.

Dolores' body was picked up by two soldiers and placed into a military truck which was quickly driven away. This was the last time the Lescanos saw their daughter. The Comandante did not want her to have a proper grave for anybody to remember her by or to turn her into a martyr. To this day no one knows where the remains of Dolores Lescano were buried. Three weeks after this tragic episode, the Lescanos were freed from prison and ordered to leave Cuba. Since they had Spanish passports, the Spanish Embassy in Havana expedited their departure from Cuba to Madrid. Had the Cuban government killed Teofilo or Luisa, it would have prompted an international response, but because Dolores was technically a Cuban citizen, nothing could be done. Although the Spanish Embassy protested the murder of Dolores, the Cuban government ignored their indictment and officially referred to this "unfortunate tragedy" as an "internal affair."

When Teofilo and Luisa deplaned after arriving in Madrid they were received as heroes by the Socialist Party, now ruling the country, and by the Cortes, the equivalent of the American Congress. The members of the Cortes voted the Lescanos a generous pension. Ironically, one of the members of the Cortes was no other than Dolores Ibaturri, the fierce communist leader of the Civil War after whom Dolores had been named. She had been in exile in the Soviet Union all these years. At the age of ninety-five she returned as a hero to Spain and was elected to the Cortes by the principality of Asturias. One wonders what Dolores Ibaturri thought about the murder of Dolores Lescano by the most tyrannical communist regime in the world. Unfortunately, she was too old to visit Cuba to be able to see the bullet holes that are still visible on the wall of the Bank of Colón to see where her namesake sacrificed her life. Dolores Lescano is gone, but the bullet holes in the marble wall of the Bank of Colón still remain to this day.

A Triumph for Freedom

"The difficulty lies not so much in developing new ideas as in escaping from old ones."

John Maynard Kenyes

Lucia Arnez was truly a daughter of the Cuban revolution. Born on October 19, 1959, the year in which Fidel Castro came to power, her parents were members of the old Cuban communist party and had been heavily involved in the Revolution. "Lucy," as everyone knew her, grew up in a home full of dinner table political discussion and debate. Both of her parents, Sergio and Marina, had been assigned important positions in the new communist Cuban government; therefore, her family never lacked any consumer goods whether staples or, at times, even luxury items. The family ate exceptionally well and lived comfortably since the Soviet Union had given Cuba the equivalent of billions of American dollars in economic aid. Most of this windfall went to jump-start the Cuban economy, but some of it trickled down to reward those who had been loyal communists.

While in elementary school, Lucy, like everyone else, joined the Young Pioneers, and when she went off to high school she took the next step and became a member of the Communist Party. Lucy was a brilliant student, a straight 4.0 at graduation time. The only thing she regretted was never visiting any country outside of Cuba. The educational system indoctrinated all Cuban students to believe that the outside capitalist world was evil and that communism was the perfect form of government. Just like thousands of other Cuban teenagers, she blindly accepted the Communist Party line about the Bay of Pigs, the Cuban Missile Crisis, and the horrible things that capitalism was inflicting on the rest of the world. Of course, television and radio were heavily censored; however, Lucy suspected that she was not receiving all of the information she needed to have a well-rounded education. As in any totalitarian regime, the populace must be shielded from the truth and fed inaccurate crumbs of reality as interpreted by the Party.

Now, at last, after graduating with high honors from high school, she was awarded a scholarship to attend the University of Moscow. She had always enjoyed biology and chemistry and so planned to major in science in order to pursue a medical degree. As a little girl she had always dreamed of becoming a pediatrician for she loved children and enjoyed the idea of being able to cure the sick. For some inexplicable reason, Cuba has always produced excellent doctors, even before the communists took over power. Lucy had worked very hard to earn her scholarship not only because the University of Moscow had an excellent medical program with the latest technology, but also because she hoped that traveling to Russia might afford her an opportunity to visit other European countries.

In August 1977, the time came to say goodbye to her parents and take the Aeroflot flight from Havana International Airport to Moscow. Due to a technical problem with her aircraft, her direct flight to Moscow had to be detoured to Paris, to diagnose and repair the mechanical problem. Passengers were put up in a small Paris hotel until the next day.

She was not upset about this interruption because it gave her an opportunity to see one of the greatest capitals in the world, albeit only for a day. The first thing she did after checking into her hotel room was to find the closest boulangerie and try one of the French pastries she had heard so much about with a hot latte. She was enthralled by the busy, noisy traffic in the streets of Paris. She had never seen so many cars, seen so many people hurrying here and there, or heard so much commotion in all of her life. To her it seemed like orchestrated chaos. The streets of Havana were practically like those of an American western ghost town compared to the hubbub of the City of Lights. With only one year of French from high school, she was still able to navigate her way in Paris by bus, by Le Metro and by orienting herself to the city rues and boulevards with a map from the hotel's concierge. She was elated to be able to move freely through Paris.

While drinking her latte and observing this unique street scene, Lucy developed a terrible headache; her mind could not reconcile what she had been told about France in Cuban schools by her teachers and what her eyes were telling her. These were free people walking the streets smiling and in good spirits, in contrast with the gray, monotonous, sad lives of the people she left behind in Cuba. Although she had been raised in a privileged home absent of rationing books or the need to wait in long food lines for hours to get the basic necessities, Lucy had been made fully aware from dinner table talk that the lack of consumer goods in Cuba were a direct result of the American embargo. Immediately after her brief reverie about home, Lucy refocused back to her pastry and latte. She realized she had some pocket money her parents had forced her to take at the last minute before she boarded her plane. After exchanging the money for francs at a bank across the street, she walked down a few streets until she found a small, and from the prices in the window, expensive boutique. She decided to splurge; after all, she was on a type of holiday today. The female clerk spoke some Spanish, and Lucy emerged with a few colorful, trendy blouses and slightly shorter skirts than she was used to supplement the drab, out of style wardrobe she had brought with her from Cuba.

Late in the afternoon, the passengers from the delayed flight were transported from the hotel by bus to Charles de Gaulle Airport where four members from the Russian embassy assisted the Aeroflot flight crew to enplane the group for their trip to

Moscow. The long flight terminated at Sheremetyvo Airport, about twenty miles from the city center. On the shuttle bus to Moscow she was fascinated by the beauty of the birch trees that lined the thoroughfare on both sides of the roads. She had never seen such beautiful trees before.

As preparation for her studies in Russia, and to the pride of her parents, Lucy had studied the Russian language from the fifth grade. Initially, she found the Cyrillic alphabet impossible, but after a few lessons with a tutor, she began to manage basic Russian. Her arrival and registration at the university were easily accomplished, and since she was the daughter of legendary heroes of the Cuban revolution she was given special privileges. She had her own private room, her own bathroom, and full access to the better dining rooms.

The University proper was located in one very large skyscraper, and all the activities were conducted inside; the compactness allowed for less wasted time since everything was included under one roof, even the Library. The dormitories, classrooms, and laboratories were all contained inside this massive building. Lucy was surprised at the number of students from all over the world, many from African countries as well as from Latin America. The student body was multi-national, and she almost suffered from information overload since she was learning things about Africa and countries in South America with every new acquaintance.

The second day after her arrival, while having breakfast, she noticed a group of students looking at a bulletin board and discussing in a loud voice something about Afghanistan. She went over to them and asked what they were so concerned about. A posted message stated that the Soviet Union was deploying the 40th Army into that country, thus beginning a war that was to last from December 25, 1979 until the Soviet withdrawal on

February 15, 1989. At the time, Lucy did not have a clue how much this event would impact her later life.

As expected, Lucy did brilliantly in school and completed her studies in three years in what normally would have taken four. She was awarded her degree in science and enrolled in the prestigious University of Moscow medical school. Her sharp grasp of concepts and her almost photographic memory quickly attracted the notice of her professors, not an easy task considering the rigorous course of studies and the competitiveness of her peers.

One morning, in 1981, without any previous warning, she received a telegram from Cuba containing the worst news imaginable. Both of her parents had been killed while directing a military expedition in the Congo. Upon hearing this news, her first thought was, "Oh my God! How could they both be dead? What on earth were my parents doing in Africa?" Her red eyes were almost cried out and she walked around in a daze. She searched for an answer to these questions. One of the friends she had made at the University, another student from Cuban, went into her dormitory room and told her that Castro had to send troops to Africa in order to pay the Soviet Union in return for the amount of money it was spending to support Castro's government. Cuba had run out of sugar and other products and had no other way to repay the Soviet Union.

Russian officials would not allow Lucy to return to Cuba or to contact anyone there. She did not know at this time that her parents had already been interred in Africa. Castro's underlings did not want to let it be known that two such important members of the Communist Party had died, particularly since they had not told the Cuban people that there were Cuban troops involved in Africa.

Lucy was expected to continue her studies and just accept the fact that her parents were dead. University officials felt that the government had invested a great deal of money and resources in educating her, and she had to do as she was told. Lucy had no other choice but to comply and continue with her studies. The faculty members of the School of Medicine, aware of her tragic loss, felt that they should assign a political commissar to keep an eye on her and make sure that she followed the Party line. After consulting with the KGB and the Politburo, they assigned a popular officer and hero of the war in Afghanistan as her political commissar.

Vladimir Timoshenko was only ten years older than Lucy but a seasoned soldier who came highly recommended by General Boris Gromov, his friend and commander of the Soviet Army in Afghanistan. What nobody knew was that Timoshenko was a disenchanted veteran who resented how his men were treated upon their return to Russia, very much the way returning American soldiers felt when they returned from Vietnam. He actually had thought about defecting to the West and had applied for a diplomatic position in East Germany with the idea of crossing the border into Berlin. He had kept these ideas very close to his heart because he well knew that his life would be worth nothing if anyone knew of his true feelings.

He was disappointed when he learned of his assignment to act as a commissar for students at the University but was thrilled when he met Lucy. It truly was love at first sight. Although he had been assigned to supervise/advise other students at the University, it was obvious that he preferred to spend more time with Lucy.

After finishing up her residency in 1983, Lucy and Vladimir discussed their secret political feelings and began to make plans to defect to the United States. First, Lucy was to request permission to visit her remaining family in Cuba. This request seemed fair and justified after being away from her home for so long. Meanwhile, Vladimir was to request assignment at the Russian Embassy in Havana. This request also seemed reasonable because his commanding officer had mentioned to him that a move to Havana would be an excellent career advancement. Becoming a military attaché in a Russian Embassy was an excellent reward for a war hero such as Colonel Vladimir Timoshenko. Their planning began to pay off when Lucy was granted her wish to visit Cuba. Much to their surprise, instead of being assigned to Havana, Vladimir was assigned as military attaché in Ottawa, Canada. His fluency in English and French was the major reason for the post in Ottawa. After much discussion and soul-searching, Lucy and Vladimir decided that after they arrive at their respective destinations, Vladimir would cross the border into the United States and request political asylum.

He knew that the Americans would be delighted with much of the military intelligence he could provide to the US, and he would be able to travel through Canada since the Russian Embassy in Ottawa was know to have a relaxed policy regarding travel. Even though this plan seemed foolproof, Lucy was concerned about the danger of anybody, especially the KGB, discovering their plans. She shared her worries with Vladimir who thought that after fighting the Mujahideen in Afghanistan, anything else would be easy. Most combat experienced soldiers don't like to talk about their war experiences, and so he did not describe his brushes with death with Lucy. He appreciated her concern and tried to reassure her that he would be very careful.

Lucy received an envelope from her uncle and aunt with a legal document from the Cuban government that was required by the Soviet Union to issue the necessary permit to obtain her plane ticket. This made Vladimir happy and sad at the same time, happy because it advanced their plans but sad because he was going to be separated from the woman he so deeply loved. Within a week, Lucy was on her way to Havana, on Aeroflot flight 126. Four weeks later, Vladimir departed for Ottawa, as the new military attaché from the Union of Soviet Socialist Republics. As he entered the Soviet Embassy in Ottawa and saw the large bust of Lenin in the lobby, it reinforced his hate for communism and all of the damage that both Lenin and Stalin had done to his beloved Russia.

Vladimir wanted to act on his plan to defect to the United States as soon as possible because he suspected that events going on in Europe might initiate profound changes in the way the government in Moscow operated. He sensed the same thing when he learned that his 40th Army unit was deployed to Afghanistan on December 25, 1979. His fear that disturbing changes in policy were on the immediate horizon became a reality when in 1989 the Berlin Wall fell and communism ended in Eastern Europe.

While in Cuba, Lucy was beginning to get desperate about her defection to the United States. Initially she thought about requesting permission to visit Mexico, a country that had always been a friend to communist Cuba, and where Castro was greatly admired by the common people for his anti-American stand. While she was working out the details of her defection, something unimaginable happened. She was informed by the Cuban authorities that a very important convention of physicians from the Third World was to open in Montreal, Canada, and she was chosen to attend. Lucy could not believe her luck at the thought of being in the same area as her beloved Vladimir. Unbeknownst to Lucy, information of Lucy's trip to Montreal had already reached Vladimir at the Embassy in Ottawa, and he had already drawn up a plan for both of them to defect to the United States over the Canadian border.

On the morning of the three-day medical convention, Lucy attended the opening address and signed up for different one-hour seminars related to pediatric medicine. Meanwhile, Vladimir started to put his plan into action.

First, he made arrangements to attend the convention, which was normal procedure for an attaché. Then, he rented a car from Hertz with American plates that was scheduled to be returned to a drop off location in the United States. Ironically, he was given a discount for returning it to the car's original pick up location. Vladimir studied entrance points along the Canadian-American border, and chose an isolated section on road where he was fairly confident they would not be stopped.

The minute Lucy saw Vladimir entering the convention saloon, her heart missed a beat, but when she saw the smile on his face she knew everything was ready. They walked out of the convention, keeping a distance from each other, until they got into the white sedan and drove away. She guessed that the lack of usual supervision over her at the convention was due to her parents' reputation as heroes of the Cuban revolution and, therefore, trusted her to be a loyal comrade. He pulled the car over and, after a warm embrace, Vladimir explained his plan to head south on Canadian Route 15, cross into the United States to link up with US Route 87, and then pass by the city of Plattsburgh in New York State. That is, if everything worked smoothly when they got to the border. If everything worked as planned, they would link with Route 95 and drive straight through to Washington, D.C. where they would surrender to the FBI and request political asylum.

It was a tense moment as they approached the American border, but were astonished how easily they managed to cross without any checkpoint or immigration guards. Vladimir wondered if this road was one of the access points the KGB used to send agents to enter and spy on the United States.

After the crossing, they relaxed a bit and finally were smiling from ear to ear: they had made it into the United States! They were now in a free country where fear was not the everyday routine as it was in the Soviet Union. Vladimir calculated approximately 618 miles from Montreal to Washington, D.C. and decided to drive well within the speed limits to prevent being stopped. He estimated that somewhere between thirteen and fifteen hours, barring any unforeseen difficulties, would be a reasonable timetable. Vladimir already knew the location of the FBI building in Washington from the maps he had studied and was prepared to shock the agents when they entered to request political asylum.

After this exhausting, non-stop drive except for gas, they reached the J. Edgar Hoover building, parked the car, and walked through the main door. Again, they were surprised at how easily it was to enter this building. Two U.S. Marshals at the entrance were mildly shocked when Vladimir and Lucy asked to see the resident agent to request political asylum since something like this did not occur on a daily basis. They were quickly taken into custody and politely escorted into a private office where a group of agents had been formed waiting to question them. After they presented their passports and identified themselves, the agents were extremely excited to have two such important people requesting asylum. After a few hours of exchanging information, the agents, aware of Vladimir's and Lucy's exhaustion, decided to move them to a safe house in the suburbs of Maryland.

They remained there for almost a month, with almost daily debriefings by members of the FBI and, most importantly, by members of the Department of State and personnel from the Pentagon. All were deeply interested about Vladimir's military career, Lucy's years at the University of Moscow, and her relationship with her dead parents. When the debriefing ended, the U.S. Marshal Service created new identities for Vladimir and Lucy. From the moment after they were married by a local Justice of the Peace, with FBI agents as witnesses, they would be known as Alexander and Rosemarie Gibson. Each was issued a driver's license, a birth certificate, and American University transcripts based on their explanations of their respective educations. Passports would be issued after they established themselves in Miami, Florida, the city they requested in which to reside and which the Witness Security Program of the US Marshal service approved. To make things even easier for Alexander and Rosemarie, the Marshal Service provided them with a comfortable condo in Miami Beach, rent free, and bought them a brand new car.

After a few months, Rosemarie obtained a position as a pediatrician at Baptist Hospital, and Alexander became a professor of Languages at the Kendall facilities of the Miami-Dade Community College, not very far from where Rosemarie worked. They enjoyed their short commute to work and loved the city of Miami where they reside to this day.

Thus ended the story that brought a triumph for freedom....

The Saga of Henry W. Morgan

"Loyalty is a fine quality, but in excess it fills political graveyards."

Neil Kinnock

Larry Morgan, a mining engineer from North Carolina, and Virginia Perez, a student at the University of Havana, met during a Havana carnival party in February 1922. Soon after the party, they began the courtship that led to their marriage in Cuba a few months later. Unfortunately, Larry's family was unable to attend the wedding, but Larry promised them that they would meet Virginia as soon as he could arrange for their trip to North Carolina.

Larry and Virginia set up a small apartment on the third floor in a modest suburb of Havana. They decided to start a family as soon as possible so that they could enjoy their children while they were young. Virginia became pregnant two months after the wedding, and Larry was anxious to introduce his new bride to his family back in North Carolina. They made plans to travel north to the United States.

Virginia felt that leaving Cuba in the summer would give them enough time to visit her husband's family and return to Havana so that the baby would be born in one of the best hospitals in Havana and attended by her personal physician. They traveled by boat to Charleston, South Carolina, and from there they continued by bus all the way to Raleigh, North Carolina. After this exhausting trip, they arrived at Larry's family home at 1415 Hillsboro Street. The couple was received by Larry's family with great love and excitement over the upcoming birth of the new addition to the Morgan family.

When Larry reported back to his Raleigh-based company, his boss suggested that he should take an advanced course on the mining of copper and nickel that was going to be offered at North Carolina State College. Since these were the main minerals found in Cuba, Larry agreed to enroll in this three-month course. He and his wife anticipated a return to Cuba by the middle of September thereby allowing ample time for the birth of the baby.

Virginia fell in love with the southern hospitality shown by the community in which Larry's family was so well known. Even though she had been raised in a strict Catholic family, Virginia enjoyed the Sunday services at the First Baptist Church of Raleigh. She particularly liked the emotional singing of the hymns and the directness and sensitivity of the sermons delivered by the local preacher. She found the experience quite a revelation and promised Larry to raise their child in an environment partial to both religions and to let the child choose between the two when the time came.

After Larry completed his copper and nickel course, he flew to New York City to meet with top executives of his company to discuss future plans for mining in Cuba. Larry's business trip delayed their departure to Havana, and, as fate would have it, Virginia was rushed to Raleigh's Dixie Hospital. Early in the morning on October 27, 1922, Henry W. Morgan was born, a healthy, vibrant, eight pound, four ounce boy. Fortunately, Larry had already returned to Raleigh and was able to be present for the birth of his son. Later, when Larry retold the events surrounding the birth of his first child, he always included the detail of the gentle, fine mist that began to fall as he left the hospital. As soon as Virginia and the baby were able to travel, the Morgan family returned to Havana, again by boat, where Virginia's family received them with great excitement. Bottles of Spanish champagne were popped for the family and for Virginia's friends and neighbors who came to celebrate the arrival of little Henry W. Morgan Perez.

The early years passed quickly and Henry was ready to begin school. Virginia decided to return to the University of Havana to pursue a degree in law and after finishing her course she began practicing law in an office near their home. Virginia's family was of great help in making sure that Henry was properly educated, and they closely monitored his grades. Henry had several of his parents' physical characteristics. His hair was dark like his father, but his skin tone was a rich caramel like his mom's; his cheeks were full and he loved to smile and laugh; he inherited his mother's blue eyes that were balanced with his father's aquiline nose. His quick mind was the result of great genes from both Larry and Virginia, although Larry, in order to avoid petty arguments, always conceded that Henry got his brains from his mother. Henry turned out to be an excellent student and an outstanding athlete; he excelled in baseball, basketball, volleyball, and handball, winning many medals and trophies. His physical and survival skills were well developed as the bullies in the schoolyard quickly learned. Some schoolmates made fun of his name, calling him "Enrique" and "El Americano." He always said that his name was Henry and defended this with his fists. Being called "El Americano" did not actually bother him because he was very proud of having been born in the United States. He never had an identity problem, was proud of having an American father and a Cuban mother, and was proud of being fully bilingual in English and Spanish. He also thought it was silly to be called "Americano," when those born in Cuba and elsewhere on the continent were American. He thought it was more correct to call him "El Norteamericano," but he was careful not to suggest that.

After graduating from high school, Henry began his studies at the University of Havana. He was planning a career in engineering, most logically because his father was a mining engineer. It was after completing his first year and starting his second year at the University that the Japanese Empire launched their sneak attack on "Battleship Row" in Pearl Harbor on December 7, 1941. Two months later shocking news came from North Carolina. His parents had received a letter from the War Department requesting that Henry W. Morgan report for active duty in the United States Army. The family in Cuba knew about the Declaration of War by President Franklin D. Roosevelt, but they were not prepared for such a quick initiation of the draft. A very important point was that Henry could have claimed Cuban citizenship and avoided the draft; however, physically, mentally and emotionally, Henry felt it was his responsibility to his country of birth to fulfill his military obligation.

During his summers spent in North Carolina, he had grown to love the United States. Also, fascism in Germany and Italy ran against his grain. The words "freedom" and "democracy" were very meaningful for him. Between 1941 and 1944, millions of Americans also felt this way and many lost their lives in defending these ideals. So, after a great sendoff by his family and friends, he embarked on a journey whose outcome he could have never foreseen.

Henry spent a weekend visiting his grandparents' home in Raleigh where he discussed the possibilities of his military assignment and the job that had to be done to defend his country. His grandparents were very concerned about Henry's safety, but Henry assured them that he would not place himself in unnecessary jeopardy, full knowing that he could never hold himself to such a promise.

Henry reported to the Selective Service Office and, after a thorough physical exam, the doctor recommended that Henry should be assigned to paratrooper school. There were no Special Forces like Navy Seals or Green Berets back then; if there had been Henry would have fit right in. Henry was in outstanding physical condition and was assigned to Fort Bragg for basic training before heading off to paratrooper school.

Fort Bragg was truly a mad house with almost 1,000 men being processed daily. The troops stationed there would increase from 5,400 to 67,000 by the summer of 1941. Initially, Henry was very happy to be so close to his family and was able to visit them on weekend passes. But, after several months at Fort Bragg, he was reassigned to Camp Claiborne located in Rapides Parish in central Louisiana where he went through the most rigorous training of his life. Although the training was brutal, all of the recruits admitted to themselves that this tough gauntlet of physical and mental conditioning was going to be invaluable to them during their war assignments.

Then, on March 25, 1942, the 82nd Infantry Division was reactivated at Camp Claiborne, Louisiana, with Brigadier General Omar Bradley as commanding general and Brigadier General Matthew B. Ridgeway as assistant commander. On August 15, 1942, the 82nd Infantry Division moved to Fort Bragg and was designated the 82nd Airborne Division with the newly promoted Major General Ridgeway in command. In a brief and lucky encounter with General Ridgeway, Henry was recognized as a possible leader in the 82nd Division. This fortuitous meeting with Ridgeway proved to be significant for Henry's later advancement in the military.

After shipping out to England for more training in preparation for the invasion of Normandy, Henry achieved the rank of sergeant. He admired the English people for their courage and determination to do whatever necessary to defend their island and repel Nazi aggression. At last, orders were received to prepare for the invasion of Europe. On June 6, 1944, D-Day arrived and the 82nd was ordered to jump behind enemy lines to protect several key bridges so that Allied troops that had landed at Normandy could advance inland. After several weeks of fighting and agonizing slow advances, the main body of the invasion at Normandy linked up with the surviving paratroopers. Exhausted and devastated by the death of many of his fellow paratroopers, Henry was ordered to report to General Ridgeway who had also jumped with the Division. Henry was reassigned to Ridgeway as Special Staff Sergeant and later realized that this assignment was responsible for saving his life; he remained a Special Staff Sergeant until Germany surrender on May 5, 1945, and received several decorations for valor.

When hostilities ended in Europe, Henry was discharged and flew back to the United States landing at Mitchell Field in Long Island, New York. From there, he took the train to Raleigh to bid goodbye to his family before flying to Cuba. He received a hero's welcome at his home in Havana and planned to enjoy long deserved "R&R" at the Hotel Torres in Varadero Beach, perhaps the most beautiful beach in the world. Between daiquiris and swimming in the warm waters he began to unwind and think about his plans for the future. In the evening he went out to dinner and listen to the music at an outside club named "El Castillito." He liked this club because from the second floor balcony he could see the sea and breathe the fresh, salty air. One evening, while visiting this club, he met a lovely woman, tanned, with deep blue eyes, inherited from her Barcelonan parents. She told Henry that she had recently graduated from an all women's college in New England. To Henry's delight, she spoke fluent English, Spanish, French, and Portuguese, having majored in foreign languages. Her name was Isabel Fernandez Figueras. They started out as friends and dated frequently. After two months things started to become serious.

When Henry returned to Havana from Varadero Beach he was very excited and told his parents about this wonderful girl named Isabel. They suggested that he should visit her and her family, who also resided in Havana, and formalize their relationship. After a short courtship, Henry and Isabel were married at the Church of Santa Catalina in the Vedado section of Havana. From Havana they flew to the Island of Pines, just south of the western coast of Cuba to enjoy their honeymoon. There, they walked on the black sand beaches of the island and went swimming in the warm, aquamarine water of the Caribbean Sea.

One afternoon, during high tide, Henry went swimming in an inlet while Isabel watched from the near pier. Suddenly, Henry felt a bump on his side and saw the tail of a tiger shark. He could not remember how quickly he reached the pier, but he was sure that he must have walked on water. For a man who had parachuted into enemy territory on D-Day and survived the war, he thought this was the second luckiest event of his life. This episode became a legend told by him and members of his family for many years; of course, the story was comically exaggerated how Henry "outswam a shark."

The first few years of Henry's marriage were the happiest years of his life. He enrolled at the University of Havana to continue his studies, but he was not very happy with the political atmosphere and the militancy of the student body. Good news arrived when Isabel announced that she was pregnant; however, another letter from the United States War Department dampened his joy. He had been aware of the turbulent events in Korea, and, while reading the newspaper, learned that on June 25, 1950, North Korean troops had crossed the border to South Korea and had moved to take Seoul, South Korea's capital. The letter requested his return to active duty and to report immediately to Fort Bragg for reappointment to General Ridgeway. The 82nd Airborne had been called up one more time to prepare for action in Korea.

Henry left his family in Cuba, flew to Miami, and then went on to Raleigh and Fort Bragg. Several of his World War II friends from the 82nd had been waiting for him in Fayetteville, a very much a US Army town. General Ridgeway, now commander of the 8th Army, wanted Henry to be part of his general staff. Before shipping out to Korea, Henry and the others who had been called up received hurried specialized training. With the arrival of these badly needed reinforcements the North Korean advance was quickly stopped. Soon, the combined South Korean forces and the American contingent recaptured Seoul and pushed back the North Koreans who retreated quickly. On September 27, 1950, Seoul fell to the Americans. In December 1950, General Ridgeway was officially promoted to General of the 8th Army.

The news of Ridgeway's promotion coincided with intelligence that Henry acquired that massive Chinese intervention in Korea was occurring and that Chinese prisoners had been taken with documents proving that many Chinese divisions were joining the fighting.

After a counteroffensive, a landing in Inchon, and very serious fighting, the Americans and their allies managed to push the combined Chinese-Korean armies back to the 38th Parallel. An Armistice was finally signed ending the Korean War. On January 25, 1951, President Harry Truman replaced Douglas MacArthur with now full general and Supreme Commander, General Matthew B. Ridgeway. He remained Henry's superior officer, and, after having sharing tough times both in Europe and Korea, he was also Henry's good friend.

Meanwhile, back in Havana, Isabel had given birth to twin girls. Henry received the news in a package sent to him by his parents, containing a letter from Isabel and a box of Cuban cigars for him and his friends. He was very happy with the news but sad because he could not be there to enjoy the happy occasion. He knew that his duty was to serve his country and that he was not the only GI who had to wait to see a new addition, or additions, to his family

Henry thought that after the end of the Korean War he would be going back home to Cuba. After, again being decorated and appreciated for his leadership, bravery, and loyalty, he was prepared to meet his wife, daughters and other loved ones in Havana. Because of his exceptional leadership qualities, Henry Morgan was ordered on another mission: to go to Indochina with a group of American advisers. His duty was to evaluate the effects of the French Foreign Legion, especially the French Airborne group in their battle against the Viet Minh. This army wanted to create a country called Vietnam, know then as French Indochina.

It was early in 1954, and Henry, now 32 years old, wrote an evaluation for his superiors about the situation in Indochina. He foresaw the possible defeat of the French forces by the tough Viet Minh general, Nguyen Giap, and suggested that the United States, which was backing the French by underwriting 80% of their war expenses, should stop its financing. Henry's report predicted the defeat of the French forces. His prediction came true when the French surrendered after the bloody battle of Dien Bien Phu. Henry's report further stated that after studying the French defeats and the tenacity and military methodology of the enemy, there should be no future American involvement in this part of the world.

The war officially ended at the Geneva Conference on July 21, 1954. Indochina was divided in two countries at the 17th Parallel; one country would be called North Vietnam, the other South

Vietnam, with Hanoi the capital of the North, Saigon the capital of the South. Ho Chi Minh, General Giap, and the Viet Minh had defeated the French in an embarrassing fashion. Henry pointed out that the war was not lost in Indochina but had been lost in Paris due to the lack of French support and the politicization of the war. When Henry sent his report to General Ridgeway, Henry was not aware of the involvement of the Central Intelligence Agency in Vietnam and that the CIA had somehow obtained a copy of his report. The CIA was not at all happy with Henry's appraisal of the situation, and arranged for Henry to become involved him in a barroom brawl with an officer who had been planted by an operative of the CIA. Thanks to the intervention of General Ridgeway, Henry was not dishonorable discharged for assaulting a superior officer. The issue was defused by discharging Henry from his duties and ordering him to return to the United States to return to civilian life. Henry was more than happy to return to his family in Cuba where he would finally meet his twin daughters whom he had only known from photos.

Arriving in a Cuba ruled then by dictator Fulgencio Batista, Henry wanted to avoid the politics, simply enjoy a well deserved rest, and return to the beautiful Varadero beach community, a mere forty miles from Havana.

In spite of being in the hands of a political dictatorship, Cuba was a prosperous country where those not politically involved could live in peace, or so Henry thought. Henry had heard of an attack on the Moncada Army Camp by a group led by Fidel Castro and ninety young revolutionaries. He also knew that Castro had been released through an amnesty agreement and was in exile in Mexico. Exhausted from the military experienced as Henry was, he did not want to talk or think about revolutions, wars, or more misery for the human race. Isabel, Henry, and the girls, Rosa and

Gloria, settled into a comfortable, three-bedroom condominium near the beach in Varadero and planned to make this their permanent residence. Their parents were frequent visitors, and they spent many pleasant hours on the beach and in their condo relaxing and playing with their beautiful daughters.

Henry did not resent the abrupt way he had been dismissed from the US Army and was enjoying a military pension and earnings from his American investments. He spent many hours fishing and quail hunting at the Zapata Swamp close to the Bay of Pigs. Many of Henry's childhood friends had also moved to Varadero, especially his best friend Miguel Garcia, the boy who used to tease Henry calling him "Enrique" and "El Americano." Miguel came from a wealthy family that was very politically involved; Miguel's father had been a Senator during the previous government of President Carlos Prio Socarras, the leader who had been overthrown by Fulgencio Batista. Unbeknownst to Henry, Miguel was a member of an underground cell belonging to the "Movement 26 of July" the name coming from the day of the attack July 26, 1953 on the Moncada camp.

On December 2, 1956, the political situation in Cuba began to deteriorate when Fidel Castro and his followers landed in Oriente Province. He and the remainder of his men, sixty survived out of eighty-one, moved into the Sierra Maestra Mountains. From that moment on, the violence increased. One revolutionary commando group killed the Havana Chief of Police and, in retaliation, members of Batista's army killed members of the revolutionary cells.

During one of Henry and Miguel's fishing trips, Miguel took advantage of the fact that the two men were alone and acknowledged what Henry had suspected all along. Miguel confided that Henry, having fought against the fascists in World

War II, should understand his desire to overthrow Batista's oppressive government. He told Henry that he wanted a democratic government with freedom of the press and respect for human rights. Henry responded that he understood Miguel's frustration but had to think about his family. And, after so many years of separation, he wanted nothing more than to enjoy his family and the quiet, peaceful life near the beach in Varadero.

Henry continued with his fishing and hunting, and he also took up photography, taking many rolls of film of his twin daughters who were growing so fast. Then, tragedy hit home. Miguel Garcia was captured by Batista's police during an attack on the Presidential Palace in Havana. Miguel survived the attack, was arrested, tortured, and murdered while still in jail. The beating he received was so bad that his coffin had to remain closed during the wake. At the wake, Miguel's father embraced Henry and with, tears in his eyes, asked, "How could you have survived all your battles and my son died at his first one?" Henry was doubly upset because very few people attended Miguel's wake and burial service because many people feared of being identified, singled out, and arrested by Batista's secret police who were in attendance at the services.

The day after the funeral, Henry, alone in his boat, thought about all of the friends he had lost in the battles in France, Germany, and Korea. Although this idyllic life at the beach with his family and friends was just what he had been hoping for, he made his most difficult decision: he would join the revolution and fight against Batista in order to save his children from living a life under an oppressive government.

The next day he contacted Miguel's friends in the underground and planned to leave for the Escambray Mountains. There, a second front had been created with the intention of relieving the pressure that Batista's soldiers were putting on Castro's revolutionaries in the mountains of Sierra Maestra. The creation of this second front would cut supplies to Batista's army by dividing the island in two. When Henry arrived at the Escambray Mountains, he met Major Ernesto "Che" Guevara, Camilo Cienfuegos, and Rolando Cubela. The insurgent leaders quickly recognized Henry's skills as a military planner and organizer. His military training helped him to prepare these untested guerilla fighters for the upcoming attack on the important city of Santa Clara. After several demonstrations of his personal courage in several confrontations with Batista's soldiers, Henry was promoted to Major. "Che" Guevara resented this recognition for Henry's valor since "Che" had been the other only foreign born Major in the rebel army. The biggest battle with Batista's military forces occurred during the Battle of Santa Clara, which resulted in a resounding victory for the Second Front of the Escambray.

On January 1, 1959, shortly after the Battle of Santa Clara, Fulgencio Batista left Cuba, and the rebel armies marched from the countryside reached the capital of Havana. Henry was elated with the defeat of the dictator and also happy to be reunited with his family. The citizens of Havana received him and all of the other revolutionaries as heroes.

Victory, though sweet, is sometimes followed by disaster. Henry's happiness was short lived when he received yet a third letter from the U.S. War Department, this time stripping him of his American citizenship for having fought with Castro's group which was considered by the US government as a "foreign army." There was no doubt in Henry's mind that this plot against him was perpetrated by the CIA who never forgave him for his negative report on future US involvement in Vietnam. He felt that if the young, recently elected, John F. Kennedy ever took a position against the Vietnam War, the President's life might be in jeopardy. After several months, and to Henry's great disappointment, the Castro brothers and "Che" Guevara started to turn Cuba into a Soviet satellite. Every week, "advisors" from the Soviet Union Block began to take more and more control of the day to day operations of the country. But the last straw was the arrests and executions of Henry's compatriots from the Escambray Mountains. Anyone with non-communist tendencies or strong religious beliefs was arrested, taken to the Cabaña Fortress, and executed with "Che" Guevara in charge of the firing squads. The murder of loyal followers of the Revolution was yet another of the twists and turns perpetrated by the Castros and "Che."

One evening, when Henry, his aide, and a few members of his command were secretly meeting in a secluded ranch outside Havana, Castro's militia surrounded the ranch and everyone inside was forced to run for their lives. Some were caught by Castro's men and, under torture, revealed that Henry Morgan had organized the meeting. Henry had rushed to his home to say goodbye to his family because he knew it was only a matter of hours before he would be arrested.

He only made his way about a mile from his house when he was surrounded by a patrol of militia and taken into custody. Immediately after Henry's arrest, a kangaroo court led by Fidel Castro found Henry guilty of treason against Cuba, and he was sent to the Cabaña Fortress to be executed. Henry's aide, Major José Correa, was also found guilty and sentenced to death. Seven other co-defendants were sentenced to thirty years in prison; luckily, three of these seven men were acquitted of the charges and quickly escaped Cuba into exile. Major Morgan's driver, the man who had been tortured and who had implicated Henry was sentenced to fifteen years in jail but mysteriously died in custody a few years later. Henry Morgan's mother appealed for mercy to President Dorticos, Fidel Castro's spokesperson, but her plea was ignored. Isabel and the twins were forced to request asylum in the Spanish Embassy in Havana; Isabel had been tried in absentia, convicted of treason, and declared a traitor to the Revolution.

One early morning, Major Henry W. Morgan, American war veteran of three major military conflicts, was marched from his cell to a wall at the Cabaña Fortress for his execution. "Che" Guevara approached Henry and said, "If you kneel before me, we will shoot you so you will die quickly" to which Henry responded, "I only kneel to God." "Che" was so enraged at his response to what "Che" though was an offer of mercy that he ordered the closest soldier to shoot Henry in both knees. The soldier did so and Henry fell to the cobblestone ground in agony. Then, after giving Henry time to experience the pain of his two shattered kneecaps, "Che" upholstered his pistol and shot Henry once in the head, killing him.

As Major Henry W. Morgan fell dead, a gentle, fine mist began to fall. Instead of being buried in Arlington National Cemetery of natural causes as a decorated United States military hero, Henry Morgan's body rests in a grave in the Colón Cemetery in Havana. The saga of his loyalty to Cuba, his dedication to his military duty, and his love for his family ended in a puddle of blood in the sand of the Cabaña Fortress.

True Friends

"Friendship is a single soul dwelling in two bodies."

Aristotle

Fernando Villar and his wife, Maria Pica, emigrated from Spain to Cuba in 1932 in search of a better life; they founded an export-import company that quickly became a highly successful business. Their son, Arturo Villar was born on October 27, 1935 in Havana, Cuba, at the Quinta Covadonga Hospital. His two sisters, Aileen and Monica, pampered their younger brother from the moment he was brought home from the hospital. The three children grew very close and throughout their childhood and into adulthood were very supportive of each other.

Just about the same time that Arturo was born in the major capital, another birth occurred in the small, rural town of Jovellanos in Matanzas Province, about eighty miles east of Havana. Rafael Gomez and his wife, Serafina, were elated that a midwife delivered a healthy baby boy, Ramón Gomez, in the back bedroom on Rafael's small farm. As it turned out, Ramón would be their only child. There were some physical problems with Serafina, and, with the advice of a Havana doctor, they decided that one child had to be their only offspring so as not to endanger the lives of both mother and child. Rafael and Serafina thanked God that they as least had Ramón and realized how fortunate they were to have a beautiful boy.

While Arturo grew up in the urban, heavily congested world of the streets of Havana, Ramón grew up riding horses and performing the wide variety of chores necessary to run the farm, chores that were particularly demanding when it was time to harvest the yearly sugar cane crop. As with many Cubans, the primary source of employment and income for Ramón's family was sugar cane, and the success of every harvest was closely tied to the price of sugar in the international commodity markets. Although the United States always paid a good price for sugar, the largest American sugar mills and large American landowners were the ones who benefited the most financially; the hardest work, of course, was in the actual harvesting in the field, but the largest profits went to the final wholesalers. For decades, this "one crop system" was the bane of the Cuban agricultural economy since most of the land was dedicated to the cultivation of sugar cane. As a result, the farms produced less and less sugar cane each year due to the gradual loss of essential minerals for the plants.

Both Arturo Villar and Ramón Gomez grew up in what was called a "Republican Cuba" where prosperity and civil rights were the result of a very progressive and democratic 1940 Cuban Constitution. This Constitution guaranteed the right to private property and respect for human rights for all Cubans. In spite of some political drawbacks, the country ran relatively smoothly and experienced little political upheaval.

After Arturo and Ramón completed their elementary studies in their respective public schools, the time came for each boy to move on to high school. In August 1951, Arturo's parents decided that he would attend the well-respected La Progresiva Presbyterian School. This was a private boarding school in the city of Cardenas that had been established by a wealthy North American missionary, Dr. Robert L. Wharton. At the same time, the city of Havana was becoming a bit too dangerous because of growing political uncertainty. Ramón's parents had friends in Cardenas who would be able to keep an eye on Ramón while his parents ran the farm back in Jovellanos. La Progresiva was selected because of its reputation for outstanding educational programs, and Ramón was extremely lucky to have the opportunity to attend such a prestigious high school thanks to a scholarship program offered to children of farmers who had excelled in their elementary schools. Ironically, both Ramón and Arturo, now 16 years old, one from the big city and one from a small farm, ended up not only in the same boarding school but as roommates in the same dormitory. The beginning of a long friendship began at La Progresiva.

From the very beginning, Arturo and Ramón became inseparable friends. Although their backgrounds were quite different, they both loved sports, especially baseball, Cuba's national sport; Arturo was a pitcher, Ramón a catcher. They enjoyed basketball and volleyball as well. In basketball, Arturo, the tallest player on the team, became the center and Ramón, the faster of the two, became one of the two guards. They brought honor to the school's athletic program earning many medals and trophies. Arturo derived special pleasure in beating teams from Havana high schools because athletes representing the city schools always looked down on teams from outside the capital that were made up of "guajiros," or farm boys. Although Arturo was from the city, he was very protective and proud of his upfront, honest "guajiro" friends. Several times their team won the FAIC, the intercollegiate athletic federation medals, which were regarded as the greatest achievement for athletic accomplishment on the high school level in Cuba.

Arturo and Ramón were great athletes, outstanding scholars, and led active social lives. They belonged to the Explorers Club, a group akin to the Boy Scouts in the US but not as highly regimented. The boys went on camping trips to places like the Zapata Swamp, near the Bay of Pigs, and hiked through and explored the lush, tropical mountains of central Cuba. The most significant role of the Explorer's Club was to teach its members a love for their country and a love for the principles of freedom and democracy.

⛆ The Unstable Political Scene ⛆

During the first year of the boys' studies, Havana had become very dangerous just as Arturo's father had predicted. On March 10, 1952, political unrest became a reality when General Fulgencio Batista ousted the elected president of Cuba, Carlos Prio Socarras, in a military coup. La Progresiva had very strong religious support from Christian churches in the United States, and the school's board of directors and the leaders of the Explorers Club felt comfortable that Batista would not dare intervene in their programs. The dictator, Batista, who was cooperative with a United States that feared and opposed the spread of Communism, knew he could not survive without the full support of the US.

⛆ The Benefits of Learning English ⛆

Arturo and Ramón decided to join "The English Club," an after school program designed to help students learn and practice the English language. Students were required to take classes in English grammar, spelling, and usage as well as be willing to perform some kind of theatrical work to be delivered entirely in English. Some members chose to read poetry, some did comic sketches, others sang popular songs. Ramón Gomez chose to do comic imitations, and several times he brought the house down with thunderous laugher and applause, either because of his quick wit, the mispronunciation of a word, or his habit of overacting. Arturo Villar chose to sing the song, "My Foolish Heart," a song he had memorized by heart from listening to it played over and over on the radio. When the time came for him to sing, he started off very well; he hit the right notes and his rhythm was perfect. A few members of the audience even quietly hummed along. But, when he reached the line, "Her lips are much too close to mine," he mixed up his English pronouns and sang, "His lips are much too close to mine." The audience roared, and Arturo's face turned beet red. When Arturo realized his mistake he laughed with everyone else realizing that the audience was not laughing at him but at his grammatical mistake.

Fortunately, this ability to laugh at himself was noticed by a lovely American exchange student in the crowd named Anita Whalton. From that moment, they were often seen together at school events, and she became his loudest supporter when she rooted for the school at his basketball and baseball games. Coincidentally, Ramón also had his first teenage crush when he met Alicia Ponce at one of the English Club meetings. She had dark black eyes, and long, shimmering black hair. Alicia picked up English quicker than Ramón, and she helped him with his pronunciation and with the irregular verbs that drive any student of English crazy.

Both couples were inseparable during that school year. Unfortunately, Ramón and Alicia had to deal with a temporary separation at the end of the school year. Alicia's family had to fly to Malaga, Spain; one of her father's older brothers had unexpectedly died, and her father volunteered to take over the small but profitable textile business. When Alicia broke the news to Ramón he was devastated; the young teens in puppy love had made plans to see each other every day throughout the summer. Ramón's mind raced, "Is there any way she could stay with relatives here in Cuba?" "If she goes, when will she return?" "Will she meet another guy in Malaga and forget him?" "What if she never returns?" He could not believe the news.

In order to cheer up his best friend, Arturo convinced Ramón to play hooky. They jumped the school fence and took the shuttle bus to Varadero Beach. During their day at the beach, they had a few beers, smoked cigarettes, checked out the local girls, and smoked an occasional cigar. Playing hooky was very dangerous in those days because if the school authorities had caught them they would have been expelled. Fortunately, they were never caught, although the head custodian inquired how their faces had gotten so sun burned. They explained to him that it was from being out on the baseball field practicing, but they always suspected that the custodian knew exactly how they had gotten the sun burned.

▓ The Political Pot Starts To Boil ▓

Meanwhile, back in Havana, the political deterioration of Cuba worried Arturo's father. On July 26, 1953, Fidel Castro and a group of about eighty-five of his followers attacked the army barracks at Cuartel Moncada in Santiago de Cuba, Cuba's second largest city. This military action led was the first attempt to resist Batista's political control of the island. Militarily, the attack was a complete debacle, but this initial show of force gave Castro the necessary exposure he needed to become the leader of the Revolution. From this first attack evolved the name of the organization "Movimiento 26 de Julio," or the 26 of July Movement, committed to fight and depose Batista.

After the failure of this initial attack, Fidel Castro was captured alive, but luckily received the protection of the archbishop of the Province, Monsignor Enrique Perez Serrantes. A brief trial found Castro guilty of treason; he was sentenced to spend the next fifteen years in the penal facility on the island of Pines, a small island southwest of Cuba.

On February 24, 1955, after having taken advantage of the divisiveness among opposing political parties, Batista officially became the Cuban President. In order to bring some semblance of peace to the island, Batista signed an amnesty document which permitted Castro to leave prison but be deported to Mexico. And, as history documents, it was while Castro was exiled in Mexico that he met Ernesto "Che" Guevara, the Argentinean revolutionary. On November 25, 1956, a revolutionary force left Mexico aboard the boat "Gramma" with a group of eighty-one men to continue the resistance against Batista. The armed group landed on the island on December 2, 1956, at Las Coloradas in Oriente Province. The group of armed insurgents was quickly detected by Batista's soldiers and was almost completely wiped out. Luckily for Fidel, he and a small group of followers were able to escape, and, with the help of a guide, they eluded Batista's soldiers and trekked through a treacherous mountainous region known as the Sierra Maestra where they established a base camp for future revolutionary operations.

On May 4, 1954, a year after the attack on the Cuartel Moncada army barracks, Arturo Villar and Ramón Gomez graduated from high school and were anxious to continue their studies on the college level. Ramón's interest in philosophy and literature led him to the field of law at the University of Havana. Ramón's father had always dreamed of his son becoming a defender of the rights of underprivileged farmers. Arturo had been more comfortable with the sciences, excelling in mathematics, physics, and chemistry and decided on a career as an engineer. A second reason to study engineering was that Arturo's father was part owner of "La Rayonera de Matanzas," a textile mill in the city of Matanzas that specialized in the manufacture of rayon fiber. Unfortunately, a major in textile engineering was not offered at the University of Havana; Arturo would have to go abroad to pursue this specialty field.

The thought of separation saddened Arturo and Ramón, but Ramón understood Arturo's dilemma. In order to pursue his field of choice, Arturo simply had to leave Cuba. They promised to keep in touch by mail and phone, to see each other during summer and Christmas vacations, and communicate through Anita, Arturo's sweetheart, who now resided in Havana with her family and would keep Ramón abreast of Arturo's progress via information included in his love letters.

Arturo applied to his three favorite American universities: Louisiana State University (LSU), Georgia Institute of Technology (Georgia Tech), and Massachusetts Institute of Technology (MIT), and was accepted at all three. He decided on Georgia Tech because of its reputation as an outstanding engineering school. Why not MIT? After looking at a map, he felt that, compared to tropical Cuba, Massachusetts was "too close to the North Pole." How naïve! So, in September 1954, the two close friends parted company. Ramón, Anita, and Arturo's family drove Arturo to the airport at Rancho Bollero in Havana to see him off on his adventure to the United States.

After getting himself settled in his dormitory and orienting himself to the campus at Georgia Tech, Arturo picked up his schedule of classes and purchased his books. He met other foreign students who were trying to acclimate themselves to a different culture with different customs and, for many, a different language. Some were from Latin America, some from various European countries, and several others from the Middle East. They all wanted Arturo to join their soccer team, but he did not know anything about the sport since, ironically at that time, soccer was known or played at all in Cuba. He was willing to try, but his heart was really set on playing baseball for Georgia Tech. He soon began practicing with the varsity baseball team, and the other players and coaches were impressed with his pitching speed and control. One afternoon at practice, a coach and several teammates asked Arturo why he did not eat lunch with them since all students with athletic scholarships ate together in a reserved area of the cafeteria. Arturo said that he didn't know there was such a thing as an athletic scholarship. He then found out that Ramón could have come with him to Georgia on a full athletic scholarship. To play baseball and study in the U.S. with his best friend would have been a dream. However, Arturo understood Ramón's love for the law and his great attachment to his native land. Ramón loved Cuba with all his heart. Arturo also loved Cuba, but having grown up in Havana was more urbane and a little less passionate than Ramón.

While Arturo was enjoying his life at Georgia Tech studying and playing baseball in a peaceful, calm environment, things at the University of Havana were not as serene and calm. There were political rallies and debates about freedom and democracy; the Federacion de Estudiantes de la Universidad (FEU), or Federation of University Students, took steps to oppose Batista's regime. Violence erupted; city buses were set on fire, and one was actually thrown down the front steps of the University. The government closed the University for several weeks; then, classes resumed only to be halted again; this cycle was repeated over and over again. The situation finally became unbearable. On March 1957, the president of the FEU, José Antonio Echeverria, leading a group of thirty overly zealous students, attacked the Presidential Palace. Their plan was to actually kill Fulgencio Batista, the country's president! In the confusion, José Antonio, thinking that the attack on Batista's life had succeeded, took temporary control of the radio station Radio Reloj and announced to its listeners that the Cuban dictator was dead. In reality, the attack had failed, Batista had not been harmed, and, upon exiting the radio station, José Antonio Echeverria was shot and killed by the police.

News of this tragedy reached Arturo at Georgia Tech, and he worried that Ramón might have participated in the attack. Arturo had known José Antonio and his family from visiting Arturo's family home in Varadero Beach and had been attracted to one of Arturo's sister. Arturo called Ramón from his dormitory at Georgia Tech, and Ramón explained what had happened. Although a student at the University, Ramón told Arturo that he was not a member of the FEU directed by José Antonio and, therefore, had not been privy to any information related to the planning or execution of the attack on Batista. Arturo was relieved that his best friend had not been a part of this fiasco.

A few months later, in June 1957, Arturo returned to Cuba to fulfill a Georgia Tech requirement that involved a mandatory internship in his field before receiving his engineering degree. As a result of his father's business connection at the "Rayonera de Matanzas," Arturo started his internship as an engineering technician at their manufacturing plant. He rented a room in a home located in downtown Matanzas, close to several restaurants that catered to the bus lines that crisscrossed Cuba. The buses always stopped in Matanzas to give the travelers a chance to relax and grab a bite to eat. Arturo frequently ate his breakfast and dinner at one of these inexpensive restaurants; a free lunch was served at the plant to the engineering staff. Arturo was one of a handful of students from various American universities who was trying to fulfill the same type of internship requirements at the textile plant. This group of up and coming engineers became a close knit group and frequently drove to Varadero Beach to have a traditional Cuban dinner, play dominoes, and drink a few beers. The tourist population in Varadero had declined considerably due to frequent sabotage activities and to the aggressiveness of the revolutionary guerillas; these saboteurs were very active around the city of Santa Clara, north of the Escambray Mountains in central Cuba. In this surrealistic environment, Arturo and his friends continued their internship, but their families were very concerned because of the proximity of Matanzas to Santa Clara and the violence, less than a hundred miles away. In reality, many Cubans did not believe that Castro and his men had a chance to succeed, perhaps because of the pro-Batista propaganda that was frequently printed in the government controlled press.

Ramón phoned Arturo at the plant, told him that he would be passing through the city of Matanzas the following Monday, and that he would like to get together. When Arturo brought up the old days at La Progresiva he sensed that Ramón did not want to reminisce. Unlike their usual extended conversations, this phone conversation was surprisingly brief. They agreed to meet on Monday at the Santiago-Havana Restaurant, which was convenient to Arturo's residence. After this conversation, Arturo spent a very restless weekend wondering why his best friend had been so aloof on the phone. He did not go to Varadero Beach with his new friends from the factory but spent the weekend reading, going to Sunday Mass, and taking long walks on the waterfront boulevard of the city. Arturo wanted to know how Ramón was coping with his law studies because he knew that after the university had closed for the last time, Ramón had taken home all the textbooks he needed in order to read law at home, known in Cuba as "estudiando por la libre," or a form of independent study. Ramón would then take the necessary final examinations. Arturo was confident that Ramón would fly through these exams because of his friend's burning desire to practice law.

When Monday arrived, Arturo decided to take the day off from work and, at six o'clock in the afternoon, walked to the restaurant to wait for Ramón. As Arturo entered the restaurant he looked around for a private table, but to his surprise, Ramón was already there, sitting at a dark, isolated table in the far corner. They embraced, exchanged a few jokes as always, and decided to slake their thirsts with a few mojitos before dinner. In spite of Ramón's friendly, relaxed demeanor, Arturo sensed that something was wrong. Two good friends who had shared so many experiences together knew each other very well, much as identical twins who can sometimes sense each other's thoughts. Finally, after a moment of silence, Ramón confided that he had joined the 26 of July Movement as a courier and was on his way to the Escambray Mountains with vital information concerning the strength of Batista's troops in that area. To say that Arturo was unhappy about this news would be an understatement. While in the United States, Arturo had read some of Herbert Matthews' articles in The New York Times, but knowing about Matthews' involvement in the Spanish Civil War, Arturo did not trust him. In his articles, Matthews had portrayed Fidel Castro as a modern "Robin Hood" which was the exact opposite of what Arturo believed about Castro. Arturo suspected that the Soviet Union was secretly backing Castro financially, and what Arturo knew about Che Guevara further reinforced his beliefs that this entire revolutionary movement had something wrong about it. He shared these feelings with Ramón, but Ramón argued that the primary objective was to remove Batista from power and bring freedom to Cuba regardless of the method. Arturo agreed that the removal of Batista was of paramount importance, but Arturo did not want to replace him with another, perhaps, worse dictator.

Arturo could do nothing to persuade Ramón to change his mind. Ramón felt an obligation to do something to remove Batista, even though he knew his parents were not in favor of Castro's revolution. It seemed that Arturo's and Ramón's parents were able to see through Castro's façade. When Ramón's bus arrived outside of the café to transport him to Jovellanos to visit his family, the two young men again embraced and made plans to see each other again when Arturo returned for Christmas vacation.

A few weeks after their meeting, Arturo left for Georgia to complete his studies and obtain his textile engineering degree. He received an outstanding evaluation from the manager of the rayon plant for his work as an intern, and was offered a full-time job after graduation based exclusively on his merit.

The Political Pot Boils Over

It was the Christmas season of 1958 when Arturo arrived to a somber Havana. There was little traffic on the streets and people were staying inside their homes. Arturo anticipated that there would be a party at his home to welcome the recently graduated engineer from Georgia Tech. Instead, his father took him aside and updated him about the serious events that were occurring in the city of Santa Clara. Arturo's father had heard on Radio Rebelde, the rebel radio station, that there had been a major battle between Batista's soldiers and the Castro-led revolutionaries. Castro's men had come down from the Escambray Mountains and were attempting to cut the island in half. This tactical move would prevent the government from sending additional troops to reinforce the army that would be isolated and highly vulnerable to attack in Oriente Province.

73

News of these events had not reached Arturo in Atlanta; the American newspapers were more interested in sports and Christmas sales. The final days of the revolution did not take long because of the low moral of Batista's troops and the dedication of the rebels in their quest to remove Batista from power. On January 1, 1959, Batista, with his family and several generals, left Cuba for good and went into exile. His departure left the city of Havana open for the rebels who quickly moved in and took control of the government. After a triumphant march toward Havana, Fidel Castro and his followers entered the city on January 8, 1959.

The Aftermath

Arturo had tried to get in touch with Ramón and had phoned his family in Jovellanos. Ramón's parents did not know where their son was and had not heard from him for several months. Arturo assumed that perhaps he was marching toward Havana with the rebels and decided to be patient and wait for Ramón to call him at his home. Ramón knew that Arturo would be back in Cuba by Christmas. Then, on January 11, 18, and February 1, 1959, the popular Cuban magazine "Bohemia" delivered what was called "Edicion de la Libertad," or Liberty Edition. There were numerous photographs of the countless crimes that had been committed by Batista's men. The picture on page thirty-nine of the February 1st edition contained the ultimate shock. This photo showed the dead body of Arturo's closest and dearest friend. The caption under the picture identified the corpse, explaining that Ramón's body had been found at "El Laguito," an affluent neighborhood where other bodies had been found before. The caption further explained that Batista's secret police had been involved in this cold-blooded murder.

The news devastated Arturo who, for the first time in his life, was forced to confront death, especially the death of somebody who had been so close to him since high school. His first thought was to call Ramón's parents who already knew that their only son had been killed. When he spoke to Ramón's parents, Arturo was truly moved: Ramón's parents were trying to comfort him instead of him comforting them.

In his anger over the entire revolutionary situation, Arturo initially approved of the assembly of revolutionary tribunals that were quickly organized throughout the island and the firing squad executions of those who committed crimes such as the one committed against Ramón. But very soon, things got out of hand and many innocent victims were executed, not for committing crimes, but for ideological differences from those of the Castro brothers and Che Guevara.

With the death of Camilo Cienfuegos, the most popular of all the leaders of the revolution, who died in a mysterious plane accident, and the jailing of Hubert Matos, another hero of the revolution, communism took control of all things connected to the Cuban government. A year later, early in 1960, began the exodus from Cuba of all members of political parties and those fortunate enough to sense what was going to follow. Total control of the island by the new communist regime was accomplished with the nationalization of private businesses; the takeover of the Esso, the American oil refinery; the take over of Shell, the British oil refinery; the nationalization of all of Cuba's sugar mills; and the expropriation of all private property.

Arturo had an opportunity to talk to Ramón's parents when they stayed a few days in Havana waiting for a flight that would take them to Miami. In spite of having been the parents of a martyr for the revolution, Ramón's parents' farm was confiscated by the communists. Ramón's parents confided in Arturo that Ramón's body had never been given to them for a proper family burial and, to that day, they did not know where his body was interred. This brought tears to Arturo's eyes and to Ramón's parents' eyes as well. They asked Arturo to do all he could to try to find out more about the murder of their beloved son. For the first time amid all of this chaos Arturo realized something shocking: Ramón's parents had been oblivious to the fact that their son had been actively involved in the revolutionary underground.

Arturo promised to find out the details, and he talked to several people who were in charge of investigating crimes that had been committed during the dictatorship. However, he did not succeed in getting any helpful information; instead, he encountered an impenetrable wall of silence. No one wanted to talk. He then tried to contact reporters at Bohemia but was told that most of them had gone to Miami fearing for their lives. He did find out one very important thing; the chief of Batista's secret police who had been involved in Ramón's death had also left for Miami. General Genovevo Lopéz, his family, and several suitcases loaded with American dollars had landed in Miami three weeks after Ramón's death; the General and his family were received in the United States as anti-communists escaping communist Cuba.

Finally, it was time for Arturo, now married to Anita, his high school sweetheart, to leave the island with his parents and two sisters. Fortunately for the family, Arturo's parents had foreseen what was to come and, while Arturo was in Georgia, had sent enough money to him so that they could live comfortably in the United States when the time came to leave Cuba. Many other Cubans who lost all of their possessions in the communist takeover and made it to the United States were forced to perform different types of manual labor until they learned enough English to acquire better jobs and to enjoy better lifestyles. The exodus of this large number of political refugees from Cuba to Miami and the success stories of these hard working people are quintessential examples of what people with solid work habits and a desire to succeed can accomplish.

Arturo's family settled in the Coral Gables area of Miami, and he was able to obtain a position at a North Carolina textile mill near the town of Henderson where he and his wife lived for the next five years. Arturo could have obtained U.S. citizenship because of his American wife, yet, like many idealist Cuban refugees, he hoped that one day he and thousands of Cuban expatriates could return to Cuba. However, after the Cuban Missile Crisis in October 1962, Arturo was sure that his country had been completely lost to the communists. He decided to pursue a new career. He had majored in engineering to please his father, but now he decided to enroll at the University of North Carolina to take courses in journalism. He felt that his background in engineering and his knowledge of journalism could help him publish a trade magazine dedicated to textile engineering and other related engineering topics.

After graduating with a bachelor's degree in journalism, Arturo, Anita, and their young son, named Ramón in memory of Arturo's friend, moved to Florida and purchased a home in Fort Lauderdale to be close to his parents in Miami. Anita did not have any family; her father had been killed in Vietnam and her mother had passed away soon after her father's death. When they got settled in their new home, Arturo began his new career as a journalist and opening an office and printing press in Miami. His business prospered and his publication, Textile and Engineering World, became highly regarded as an important addition to the specialty trade magazines of the engineering profession.

One evening, while Arturo was relaxing at home playing with Ramón, he tuned on his favorite Spanish-speaking television station. The program he preferred was a discussion panel led by the distinguished moderator Oscar Haza, who, although originally from the Dominican Republic, had extensive knowledge of Cuban history and Cuban politics. The program consisted of a panel of military and political members of Batista's regime who were there to clarify some of the misinformation the Cuban communist government was spreading in the United States. Some of the panelists mentioned the progress made in Republican Cuba citing improvements in the economy and describing the prosperity they had left behind. They acknowledged the stupidity of Batista in not allowing more freedom to the Cuban people, and they blamed the United States for perpetuating Batista's regime as a buffer against communism. The old saying, "The enemy of my enemy is my friend," ironically left the door open for the communist takeover of Cuba.

The moderator introduced the fourth panelist as, "General Genovevo Lopéz who had been the Chief of SIM (Service of Military Intelligence) during Batista's reign." Arturo jumped out of his chair when he heard General Lopéz's remarks. Lopéz began to explain the murder of Ramón Gomez who had been tortured and murdered during the last days of the revolution by one of Batista's repressive groups. The General stated that a telephone call had been received in his office. The anonymous caller stated that the leader of the underground in Havana was Ramón Gomez and that he could be located at the FOCSA apartment building, unit 2627, in the Vedado section of the city. A group of Batista's soldiers was dispatched to the building, found and arrested Ramón, and brought him to the SIM headquarters where he was tortured and finally murdered for not revealing the location of his friends. Arturo knew that it was Vilma Espinosa, not Ramón, who had been the real leader of the underground in Havana. She hated Ramón because of his religious beliefs and his strong anti-communist sentiments. When she felt that Batista's men were getting too close to identifying her hiding place, she decided to betray Ramón to take the attention away from her. Thus, Ramón became the second patriot caught in the web of international Communism. The first patriot who had been betrayed was Frank Pais, the leader of the underground in the city of Santiago de Cuba. He had organized the military ruse that allowed Castro to land in Cuba and march to the Sierra Maestra mountains to start the revolution from there. Frank Pais was betrayed by a different woman, also named Vilma, her "nom de guerre," for his religious beliefs and strong anti-communist beliefs, just like Ramón. Frank was an extremely popular leader, and Fidel was so jealous of Frank's popularity that he could not endure it. Fidel planned to have Frank eliminated. Vilma called the Army headquarters in Santiago de Cuba and gave them the exact location of Frank's hiding place. After Frank Pais was murdered, thousands marched to the cemetery for his burial. Thus, Ramón became the second patriot caught in the web of Cuban communism.

Arturo was glad that his family had relocated from North Carolina to southern Florida because in North Carolina they did not have access to news from Cuba. He also, in a sad way, felt relief in the fact that Ramón, who gave his life in the fight for freedom and democracy, did not live to see the destruction of his beloved Cuba at the hands of international communism. Arturo, the pragmatist, was forced to go abroad to study textile engineering to please his father. He could just as easily have ended up studying in Cuba, and who knows what could have happened to him? If it had not been for his selection of that one particular college major, Arturo could also have been swept up in the political scene and met the same fate as his beloved friend Ramón. The one thought that kept going around and around in Arturo's mind for the rest of his life was, "Why him and not me?"

Gustavo Garcia Martinez (GGM)

"We tell our triumphs to the crowds, but we are the sole confidants of our sorrows."

Robert Bulwer-Lytton

Guatemala is a small country in Central America, strategically located bordering Mexico, Belize, Honduras, and El Salvador. In 1951, Colonel Jacobo Arbenz Guzman and his regime succeeded the government of President José Juan Arebalo. Immediately after assuming power, Colonel Guzman implemented liberal policies; for one, he instituted an agrarian reform law to break up large estates in order to foster highly productive individually owned small farms. This reform policy was strongly supported by Guatemala's Communist Party, and, because the source of this support was from the Communists, the United States' Central Intelligence Agency kept a close eye on how these reforms would affect Guatemala's future political position.

One of the most significant aspects of the land reform was the breaking up of the United Fruit Company, a huge banana plantation that was owned, in part, by the United States Secretary of State, John Foster Dulles. In 1953, the Guatemalan government also appropriated 225,000 acres from the United Fruit Company and turned it into public land.

During his presidency, Jacobo Arbenz Guzman allowed the communist Party to freely organize and included leftist leaders among his top advisers. While this political activity was occurring in Central America, the United States government was fighting Communist forces in Korea as well as trying to cope with Communist influence in Eastern Europe and other Asian "hotspots." In May 1954, as arms from Eastern Europe began to arrive in Guatemala, the United States, fearing that the Guatemalan government was going to turn Communist, decided on a plan to overthrow Jacobo Arbenz's government.

During this charged atmosphere in Guatemala, an Argentinean trained medical doctor, Ernesto Guevara, arrived in Guatemala

City and met Nico Lopéz, a Cuban veteran of the Moncada attack where Fidel Castro began the revolution against the Cuban dictator Fulgencio Batista and both became good friends. Guevara had already met with some survivors of the Moncada attack while he was living in Costa Rica.

Ernesto Guevara interviewed for a job at a leftist newspaper in Guatemala City and had a fortuitous meeting with Gustavo Garcia Martinez, a young reporter with aspirations of becoming a professional writer. Gustavo had written several short stories and a few brief articles for the newspaper, but he frequently lived from hand to mouth having to borrow money from friends and family to pay rent for his small apartment and for food. A sincere rapport developed between Ernesto and Gustavo based on their mutually shared interest in Marxism and their concern for the world's disenfranchised common people.

However, their friendship was interrupted on June 17, 1954, when CIA mercenaries invaded Guatemala and, through a successful propaganda campaign, convinced the Guatemalan citizens that they had a much larger force than they actually had. Ernesto Guevara attempted to organize a civil militia, but senior army officers blocked the distribution of weapons, and President Jacobo Arbenz was forced to resign and escape to live in exile in Mexico. Colonel Castillo Armas became President of Guatemala and remained president until his assassination on July 26, 1957. By this time, Ernesto Guevara had already been singled out as a communist and also had to escape to Mexico. Gustavo Garcia Martinez, now called "GGM," who still had an ambition of becoming a great writer and who had managed to publish some of his short stories while in Mexico, accompanied him.

Soon after Fidel and "GGM" arrived in Mexico, Ernesto Guevara, now called "Che," met with Raul Castro and his brother

Fidel, and they became close comrades. Che joined the Castro brothers in their revolutionary efforts to overthrow the dictatorship of Fulgencio Batista in Cuba. Meanwhile, "GGM" established a deep friendship with the leader of the movement, Fidel Castro Ruz, and pledged his support through his writings that appeared in the Mexican newspaper. Castro and his group counted on the anti-American feelings in Mexico and on November 25, 1956, at 11:00 PM and, as history can attest, it was from the town of Tuxpan on the east coast of Mexico that 82 men headed for Cuba on the yacht "Gramma" to begin what would turn out to be the beginning of the end of the Batista regime in Cuba.

At this time the Cuban populace were totally unaware of Castro's group's involvement with the Soviet Embassy in Mexico. Also, the recruiting of Che, the monetary support of the Soviet embassy, and the training of the men by a communist Spanish civil war general would have sent "red flag". It seemed that the Cuban people were more concerned with liberating the island from their dictator, Fulgencia Batista, than in securing their government from Soviet influence. Another warning sign that something was amiss was when Herbert Matthews, correspondent for The New York Times, visited Castro in Cuba's Sierra Maestra Mountains. The Cubans where not aware of Matthews' leftist tendency. When he had been a correspondent in the Spanish Civil War, his stories were filled with misinformation, favorable to the Republican side, to the American people.

Meanwhile, "GGM" continued to write numerous newspaper and magazine articles glorifying the heroic rebels that were fighting in Cuba. He also sent letters to Fidel in the Sierra Maestra Mountains emphasizing his total support for Fidel's cause and informing him of the popularity that his revolution was gaining around the world. After having achieved his dream of becoming a popular commercial writer in Mexico, "GGM" secluded himself for several months in a tiny apartment and wrote his first full-length novel entitled El Arbol, Spanish for "The Tree." Set in rural Guatemala, the book detailed the life of an impoverished farmer's family that had been abused for years by their tyrannical landlord. Ironically, "GGM" came upon the idea for the plot from casual conversations he had had with Fidel Castro prior to Fidel's departure for Cuba. Fidel had told him of the abuses his own father had committed with his laborers at their Cuban farm in Oriente Province.

From 1955 on, "GGM" wrote a book every two or three years and began to be recognized as a writer with strong political messages. Although a Marxist by faith, he was never officially classified as a communist, and he was very careful in maintaining a correct line. He thought of himself as a spokesman for the underprivileged and politically unrepresented common man.

When Fidel Castro and his rebel army marched in triumph into Havana, "GGM" was photographed standing in front of the Presidential Palace, applauding and embracing his friends Fidel Castro and "Che" Guevara. From that moment on, "GGM" became a permanent guest and almost a living shadow of Fidel. Fidel arranged for the best living arrangements for his political mouthpiece. "GGM" was accommodated in a luxurious home complete with an in-ground swimming pool and landscaped gardens in the exclusive Miramar section of Havana; the refrigerator was always stocked with the best food available, and he was given a new Mercedes-Benz. Of course, "GGM's" "property," as well as the properties of many other friends of Fidel, had previously belonged to wealthy Cubans whose property had been usurped, without any compensation, by the communist regime led by Fidel. Many upper-class Cubans who had suspected what was coming for Cuba and already left the island, while other successful businessmen who were not as prescient, had their homes and businesses forcibly confiscated by the new communist government.

Frequently, Fidel would arrive at "GGM's" house with his bodyguards late in the night unannounced and, between coffee and cigars, their conversations would continue into the early morning hours. Fidel encouraged "GGM" to write a "super" novel that would make Fidel internationally known. He discouraged "GGM" from writing about the Cuban revolution but, instead, encouraged him to write about his own country, Guatemala. Castro emphasized that Guatemala had suffered so much from the abuses of the United Fruit Company and the CIA's involvement, that Guatemala had been prevented from becoming the first Marxist country in Latin America. During these personal, often clandestine conversations, "GGM" was very careful not to confront Fidel about the brutal methods he was using to secure his control of the island, but he did inquire about the execution of many of Fidel's original followers at the hands of the firing squads run by Che at the Cabaña Fortress. To these carefully worded inquiries, Fidel jokingly responded, "There is a saying, 'To make an omelet you need to break some eggs.'" Fidel continued, "Besides, they were counterrevolutionaries who refused to follow the principles of the revolution, and by that I mean the Marxist revolution." When "GMM" asked Fidel about the exceptional number of Cubans that were fleeing the island, Fidel compared this with the expelling of the non-Christians from Spain after the re-conquest and further stated that, "Those who don't believe in our revolution we have to let them go. By their leaving there will be no opposition to our regime." After several of these very sensitive discussions, "GGM" decided it would be in his best interest to avoid these topics; however, he did managed to persuade Fidel to free and send into exile several newspaper writers and intellectuals who had been his friends before the revolution.

These late evening conversations continued sporadically but two weeks would not go by without a knock at "GGM's" door late at night for another round of political discussion, coffee, and cigars. They sometimes discussed many of the events that occurred in Bogota, Colombia in 1948 where Castro went as a representative of the University of Havana. They marveled at the coincidence that their paths had crossed during one of the political events in Bogota and even recalled the clothing that they were wearing at that time when "GGM" had been in Bogota working as a free lance reporter for a Guatemalan newspaper. Both young men had been in their twenties, and both were exploring Marxist ideas. The discovery that they both had Marxist sympathies strengthened their relationship. However, many of "GGM's" old friends began to distance themselves from him exactly because of his new political interests. His friends could not understand how a man so concerned with the plight of the poor could not acknowledge the miserable situation of the Cuban people under communist rule and how Castro was essentially selling their beloved country to the Soviet Union.

Following Fidel's suggestion, "GGM" returned to Mexico City, rented another small, one bedroom apartment, locked himself in seclusion for a second time, and wrote what would turn out to be his masterpiece: Too Many Years of Submission, which chronicled the abusive strategies of large American corporations and their capitalistic obsession for profit in the Third World. The plot sounded very much akin to what had happened in Guatemala with the United Fruit Company. He dedicated the first copy to his friend, Fidel Castro Ruz, who expressed great admiration and approval for the novel in his marathon political speeches and in the Havana press. A few years later, in 1982, the Nobel Prize Committee, continuing with a noticeable pattern of rewarding controversial socialist authors, awarded "GGM" the Nobel Prize for Literature, thereby making Too Many Years of Submission an international best seller. After "GGM" received the award, Fidel invited him to give seminars on literature and cinema at the University of Havana. Fidel's plan was to use "GGM's" notoriety from his literary award deliberately as a propaganda tool so as to lure college students from many Latin American countries to travel to Cuba to study and to learn about Marxism. At the same time, Cuba was receiving billions of dollars from the Soviet Union that helped to create a sense of economic normalcy to the island.

With the Bay of Pigs and the Cuban Missile over, this apparent economic normality did not reach the common Cuban citizen. "GGM" continued to live in his mansion in Miramar and continued to have the usual night time "literary" conversations with Fidel Castro who because of doctors' orders, was no longer allowed to smoke cigars but still continued to drink wine and rich Cuban coffee.

During another of their conversations, Fidel's explained his reasoning for ordering the sinking of the tugboat "13 de Matzo" in Havana's harbor. Many women and children drowned, their only crime being to try to leave Cuba in search of freedom. Fidel perceived that this attempt to leave Cuba now was an affront to his authority and to his enormous ego.

Still another issue that seriously disturbed "GGM" occurred later in 1996 when Fidel ordered the shooting down of two unarmed planes operated by "Brothers to the Rescue," piloted by American citizens whose mission was to rescue Cubans escaping on rafts in international waters. At this time he also recalled when Fidel explanation to "GGM" was that it was a test to see how the United States would react. Castro predicted that the Unites States Air Force squadron stationed in Key West would do nothing. His prediction proved absolutely correct, and the heinous crime of shooting down unarmed civilian planes perpetrated by Fidel remains unpunished to this day. There was a great deal of protest at the United Nations, but nothing concrete developed. After listening to Fidel's explanations of these political actions cited above, "GGM" became disillusioned and decided to go to Mexico City, and Fidel took "GGM's" leaving Cuba as an affront to his authority.

"GGM" continued to reside in Mexico City, instead of his native Guatemala City, because of the bloody thirty-five year old war with weapons supplied to the guerrillas from Castro's Cuba. Guatemala became a country with the world's highest murder rate with very little consequences or convictions. In the fall of 1999, "GGM" traveled to the United States to seek treatment for an undisclosed cancer. Ironically, he chose not to obtain medical help in Cuba, whose government was always boasting about their excellent medical care. His decision to go to the United States was very surprising to those who knew him because it was he who considered himself an anti-imperialist and criticized any intellectual who traveled to the United States. As soon as he arrived in Los Angeles, he contacted the local FBI Office and arranged for a meeting in a reserved area of the hospital for VIP patients. At the FBI headquarters, the name Gustavo Garcia Martinez was immediately recognized as Fidel Castro's closest friends. Actually, more than a friend, he had been a close confidant who had been loyal to him for many years. The FBI had kept an extensive dossier of "GGM's" activities and immediately dispatched two Special

Agents, Peter C. Martinez and Arlene Allen, to interrogate him. Both agents were American born but of Cuban descent raised in Miami and fully bilingual. They arrived at the LA hospital and met with "GGM." At first, they thought that he was going to ask for political asylum, but they certainly were not prepared for what was going to transpire during the interview.

Without hesitation, "GGM" began to explain to them the reasons for his call. He told them, "I am extremely disappointed with what is going on in Cuba and would like, in any way possible, to help you with information as to what is going on in Fidel Castro's Cuba. I know it sounds odd to behave as a counter-revolutionary after many years believing that socialism was the answer to the problems of the poor countries, and I don't want to totally discredit socialism, but what goes on in Cuba is nothing less than totalitarianism, the most brutal form of communism." He further added, "I stayed this close for so long to Fidel with the intention of saving some of my intellectual friends from extended jail terms, and I have in some ways accomplished this goal."

After carefully listening to "GGM's" story Agent Martinez suggested that they should contact the CIA which may be the appropriate United States agency to pursue this issue. Upon hearing Agent Martinez's suggestion, "GGM" became very agitated and expressed his strong opposition to such a plan. He explained that the CIA had a terrible track record not only in earlier events in Guatemala, but also in the handling of the Bay of Pigs invasion. He believed very strongly that the CIA was infested with informants who kept Fidel up-to-date with what was going on in the Agency.

After several days of deliberations, top decision-makers in the FBI decided to go along with "GGM's" desire to keep this exclusively under the aegis of the FBI. They requested that "GGM" should deliver any pertinent information to an undercover agent working in Havana. "GGM" could not believe that this agent in Havana was no other than the individual in charge of pool maintenance and landscaping of the property given to him by the Cuban government in Miramar. As a matter of fact, this agent had also been responsible for keeping his refrigerator well stocked and had authorized the installation of a gasoline operated generator to supply electricity to "GGM's" house due to the frequent power outages in Havana. This undercover agent would pass information to the FBI using pre-selected tourists and families returning to the United States after visiting relatives in Cuba.

Upon completion of his cancer treatment at the hospital and after getting a satisfactory report, "GGM" left for Cuba via Mexico. He arrived in time to hear Castro's plans to demand the return of Elian Gonzalez by the U.S. Government. Elian was the little boy who lost his mother while both crossing on a raft through shark infested waters between Cuba and Key West trying to reach freedom. This tragedy began on November 22, 1999, and it took until April 22, 2000, at which time the U.S. Attorney General, Janet Reno, with the help of the Immigration and Naturalization Service, forcefully removed Elian from his family's home in Miami. Elian had been living with them since the Coast Guard rescued him. Fidel boasted to "GGM" that he knew that this raid was going to take place before it happened. This left "GGM" asking himself, "How did Fidel get this information?" "Was Janet Reno's office infiltrated by a Castro spy or spies?" "GGM" passed this sensitive material to his FBI connection and continued passing on information to the FBI in the years that followed. Some of these reports included the case of the seventy-nine intellectuals and internal dissidents who, on March 18, 2003, were sentenced to as many as twenty-eight years of imprisonment. Their only crime was to demand freedom of speech. Fidel took advantage of the U.S. Government's preoccupation with the Iraq war to accuse these men of crimes against the state and to imprison them simply to get them out of his way.

On April 11, 2003, Fidel ordered the execution of three young Black men who were caught trying to escape Cuba. The sentencing of the seventy-nine intellectuals and dissidents, and the execution of the three Black men would have never been known to the world if it hadn't been for "GGM's" reports to the FBI. The FBI leaked these events to the local press, and these atrocious crimes were reported in the international press. "GGM" tried to persuade Fidel not to imprison the seventy-nine intellectuals, but Castro would not listen to him. He wanted to set an example for any other dissidents on the island.

The most important information passed by "GGM" to the FBI was the news that Fidel Castro was gravely ill. Long before the world was informed of Fidel's undisclosed intestinal disorder, John D. Negroponte, Director of the National Intelligence Agency, had been briefed by the FBI concerning Fidel's illness. Cuban Internal Security was extremely upset about this leak regarding Fidel's deteriorating health and tried very hard to determine its source since Fidel's illness was considered a closely guarded "state secret." "GGM" sensed that Raul Castro, Fidel's younger brother, suspected that the leak was coming from someone close to his brother.

As Fidel's health worsened, Raul took more and more control of the government's daily operations. Raul never really liked "GGM" and was actually jealous of the close relationship that "GGM" shared with his own brother. The situation became too precarious for "GGM" as Fidel's health deteriorated. Who was going to protect him from Raul once Fidel was completely out of the picture? It would only be a matter of time before there would be another knock on his door in the middle of the night but this time it would be Raul or a squad of soldiers sent by Raul to eliminate him. "GGM" decided that it was time to leave Cuba and return to Mexico City. He knew that this time his close friendship with the "Maximum Leader" must come to an end.

No one will ever know "GGM's" true feelings regarding his extremely close relationship with Fidel. For almost four decades many Cuban expatriates living in the United States and elsewhere have criticized his loyalty to Fidel. During the summer of 2005, "GGM" moved to the United States permanently because Mexico was not safe; he feared an assassination attempt on his life. Cuban Security was very active in Mexico and frequent kidnappings were occurring throughout the country. Just as Josef Stalin had arranged for the August 20, 1940, elimination of Leon Trotsky in Mexico by Ramon Mercader, a Russian agent, so Fidel could easily arrange for a similar fate to befall "GGM" by one of Fidel's trusted henchmen.

Ironically, Gustavo Garcia Martinez, a man who had literally been one of Fidel Castro's right hand men and confidants, decided to make his permanent residence in the country that he had hated all his life: The United States of America.

Wings of the Revolution: A Pilot's Story

"You measure a democracy by the freedom it gives its dissidents, not the freedom it gives its assimilated conformists."

Abbie Hoffman

While flying on a top security mission over the Caribbean Sea on his way from Costa Rica to the Sierra Maestra mountains in the southeast section of Cuba, Roberto Lance was worried about the narrow landing strip awaiting him. The strip's landing area was cut out from what had been a rough sugarcane field. Roberto was the only pilot working for the rebels led by Fidel Castro, and he knew the importance of his mission in the struggle to overthrow Fulgencio Batista's dictatorship. Roberto also knew of Castro's faith in his skill as a flyer and his loyalty to the revolutionary movement. In a show of bravado, he painted on the side of his single prop plane, in red letters: "26 de Julio" to honor the date Fidel Castro and his revolutionaries attacked the Moncada military camp in the city of Santiago de Cuba located in Cuba's Oriente Province.

Roberto had left Punta Arena, Costa Rica, on March 1958, with his plane loaded with weapons and ammunition that would help in bringing an end to the political struggle. Roberto, the product of a wealthy family with a distinguished background in local and island-wide politics, was raised to be political aware and political active. In fact, Roberto's grandfather, Don Luis Lance Lopéz, had fought for Cuban independence in the 1890's against Spanish colonial soldiers. Roberto's background was in sharp contrast with that of his compatriot, Fidel Castro, who had been born into a farmer's family with limited financial resources and little or no interest in politics.

Fidel Castro was born in Oriente Province on August 13, 1926, while Roberto Lance entered the world just under three months later in Havana on November 8, 1926. They met for the first time as students at Belén Jesuit Preparatory School, a prestigious institution that had been founded in 1854 in Havana;

the faculty was comprised of Jesuit priests and brothers, a religious order that was known for its high standards of academic excellence and long years of success at instilling religious discipline in their students.

Roberto and Lance formed a close relationship based on several similar personality traits, one being the desire to excel at whatever endeavor to which they applied themselves.

One humid afternoon while at baseball practice Roberto told Fidel that, as a child, he had always wanted to fly airplanes. Fidel replied, "I hope you will be as good a pilot as I am a pitcher." Ironically, this worried Roberto because he did not think much of Fidel's ability on the baseball diamond, either as a pitcher or a hitter. If Lance couldn't fly a plane better than Fidel pitched Lance knew that he would be in serious trouble in a plane. They parted company after graduating high school, Fidel advancing to the University of Havana to study law, Roberto enrolling in an aviation school where he subsequently graduated in 1944 with a major in aviation mechanics and his pilot's license. Although each had gone off to different schools, they always kept abreast of what the other was doing, and Fidel felt especially proud when Roberto told Fidel that he had received an appointment as a co-pilot for the Cuban airline "Aerovias Q," flying the Miami, Florida/Havana, Cuba route. Although he had not been involved in the revolution from its inception, Roberto met with leaders of the underground in Havana and offered his services to the revolution as a pilot. When Fidel learned that Roberto was interested in joining the revolution he was elated. Fidel knew he was going to need a pilot who could be trusted implicitly to deliver arms to Fidel's mountain hideout. At the beginning of most revolutionary movements, insurgents have limited weapons, and, for Fidel, it was the same. Not only did Fidel lack adequate weapons; there was absolutely no way to traverse from the Maestra mountains with a force large enough to attack Batista's well-trained, well-disciplined soldiers without proper arms.

Knowing that inferior weaponry hopefully supplied by an almost non-existent delivery system constituted an almost insurmountable problem, Roberto proceeded to purchase weapons and ammunition on the black market in Miami. Roberto bought an F-51D-30NT airplane from Leeward Aeronautical Sales, and picked up an F-51-30-NA plane from the ex-Royal Canadian Air Force which had also been advertised for sale in the Miami area. Unfortunately, a Curtiss C-46 Commando aircraft Roberto had previously rented in Miami for $2,000 was damaged beyond repair when he attempted to land at a short, poorly prepared landing strip in the Sierra Maestra mountains.

Unknown to Fidel, some of the weapons intended for the insurgents were sent to Havana and Varadero on the Cuban National Airline, Cubana de Aviación, because several rebels had infiltrated the airline and compromised the security thereby making it relatively easy to smuggle weapons into Cuba for the cause. Most of these weapons ended up in the Escambray Mountains of Central Cuba where the rebels had established a Second Front. As it turned out, this "second front" was the one that brought final defeat to Batista's troops and ended the revolution.

Roberto had flown many missions to deliver military supplies from Venezuela and, perhaps as many as 70% of the weapons delivered to Castro came from Roberto's dangerous runs. However, not all attempts to smuggle weapons into Cuba were successful. On November 1958, a band of Cuban rebels hijacked a turbo-propeller Viscount airplane from Cubana de Aviación, originating from Miami, loaded with a large cache of weapons.

The hijackers had originally intended to land on a small landing strip close to the Preston Sugar Mill in Oriente Province. The plane was unable to land at this airstrip because Batista's soldiers had blocked the airfield with steel drums, heavy industrial dump trucks, and backhoes. To land the plane and be captured would be suicide. The five insurgents on board had no choice; they ordered the pilot to abort the landing. Unfortunately for all passengers, the plane, which was loaded with materiel critical to Castro's plans, ran out of fuel and crashed into the Bay of Nipe on the north coast of the Oriente Province. Innocent civilians on this flight died in the plane crash as a result of being caught up in the foiled plans of the hijackers; the rebels onboard, who knew about the potential dangers inherent in any attempt to hijack a plane, lost their lives attempting to transport needed military weapons to bolster the military strength Fidel's forces. To think, only months later, victory would come to the revolutionary forces and the dictator, Fulgencio Batista, would end up being forced into exile on January 1, 1959.

Roberto flew from Havana to the city of Camaguey to try to persuade Batista's Air Force pilots to stop serving the dictator and join the revolution. Roberto gave his word that Fidel would protect their lives, and, after discussing the offer amongst themselves, the pilots decided to join the revolution. Roberto learned that he had been appointed by Fidel to be the chief of the newly created Revolutionary Air Force. Accompanied by the new Air Force Chief, these pilots returned to Havana expecting to contribute their important skills to the revolution. However, upon arriving at the Columbia military camp, the pilots were arrested by order of the also new Join Chief of Staff, Raul Castro. Roberto protested to Raul but to no avail. In spite of Roberto's verbal promise of safety, many pilots who were willing to reject Batista and embrace the revolution ended up either in a jail cell or executed in the Cabaña Fortress. Ernesto "Che" Guevara, Fidel's appointed comandante of the Cabaña Fortress, ordered the executions. The jail sentences and executions continued in spite of an order of amnesty given by the "Maximum Leader," Fidel Castro.

The loss of the men on the hijacked Viscount plane and the treatment of the pilots were the first of many disappointments suffered by Roberto Lance and marked the beginning of his loss of confidence in the Castro revolution. In spite of this loss of confidence, Roberto remained as Chief of the Revolutionary Air Force from his sense of commitment and duty. Many of his closest friends criticized his decision to remain as Chief and thought that he should have resigned immediately. Roberto was similar to many Cubans who initially would not accept the fact that Fidel was not keeping any of his early promises with respect to human rights, freedom of the press, and free elections. In reality, Roberto decided to remain in his powerful position in order to save the lives of not only the remaining Batista's pilots, but also of the technicians who took care of the airplanes. Unfortunately for all men included in Roberto's plan, it was thwarted with an unexpected confrontation with Fidel.

The showdown began when Roberto opposed the placing of old guard communists into the principal positions in the new government. When he broached this topic with Fidel, a heated argument erupted between the two; Fidel was in no mood to have his political directives questioned in front of others. As a result, Fidel told Roberto that as of that moment he was no longer Chief of the Revolutionary Air Force. Roberto was lucky that his questioning of Fidel's policy didn't cost him his life. Only one other member of the rebel army, a surviving member of the Battle of Santa Clara and a patriot loyal to the Revolution, had questioned Fidel's policies in front of his associates at the Presidential Palace. This member, like Roberto, was lucky that he was not sent to the Cabaña Fortress. In fact, his friend, who had been an aide to "Che" Guevara, was subsequently warned to get out of Cuba before he was arrested, and, with the help of the American Embassy, the friend and his wife managed to escape and fly to Miami.

Roberto did not need such warning. In June of 1959, he took his wife and their three children to Varadero Beach and launched his sailboat, destination: Florida. In spite of bad weather, they arrived in Miami on July 4, 1959. Hence, Roberto and his family became some of the early "balseros," those who escaped Cuba by sea. Of course, many more Cubans were to attempt the dangerous voyage just to escape Castro's Cuba. Some made it; others whose improperly constructed vessels were not truly seaworthy lost their lives in the shark-infested waters between Cuba and Florida's and never made it to Florida's southern coast. Still, there were others who launched their boats but were captured by Fidel's shore patrols and returned to Cuba to face imprisonment, torture, or execution for being disloyal to the cause.

Upon reaching Miami, Roberto Lance did not sit down and lament about his predicament, jobless, and with a family to support. On the contrary, he immediately volunteered to testify before the U.S. Congress about how Cuba was being transformed into a communist country Soviet aid. He attended congressional meetings accompanied by other Cuban dissidents residing in North Carolina who supported his position. Remember that this occurred in 1959, at a time when many Americans considered Fidel Castro as a hero and were ignorant as to what was really going on in Cuba.

Meanwhile, Roberto continued his political activism in North Carolina to thwart Fidel's communist government by flying airborne sabotage missions over Cuba. The goal was to deliver arms and ammunition to groups who were organizing a counter-revolution in the mountains of central Cuba. Roberto also flew over Havana in a B-24 to drop leaflets accusing Fidel of betraying the original precepts of the revolution and turning the island into a Soviet satellite. Later, Castro falsely accused Roberto of dropping bombs on Havana. Had the Cuban government not been so preoccupied with its plan to consolidate power, Roberto Lance would have been marked for extermination by Cuban agents who were already in place in the Miami area, as well as in other major United States cities.

Fidel was furious at Roberto Lance's defection to the United States and decided to extract a perverted type of revenge. Another popular leader of the rebel army was Hubert Matos. After Lance's escape to the US, Matos was arrested and send to prison for thirty years for his presumed association with Lance. It seemed that Castro had a vendetta against anyone whom he considered more popular than he. Another popular rebel leader, Camilo Cienfuegos, mysteriously disappeared, vanishing during a flight from Camaguey where he had met with Hubert Matos. These events, together with the death of Ernesto "Che" Guevara in Bolivia years later, left Fidel Castro as the only leader of his revolutionary government.

Meanwhile, in Miami, Roberto Lance created the first organization to represent the opposition to the communist takeover in Cuba. With a large Cuban migration from Cuba to the United States, primarily to Miami, Cuban expatriates began to establish themselves as a minority with a resolute political voice. With so many Spanish-speaking residents in Miami, one did not have to be fluent in English in order to succeed in business. Several radio stations at least one television station began to offer programs in Spanish. The problem was, and, to this day, is, that Cubans grew more frustrated than ever at the realization that they had lost their country and that not one of the major US political parties, neither Republican nor Democrat, was going to do anything to remove communism from their beloved island.

It was in 1962, soon after the disaster of the Bay of Pigs invasion and after President John F. Kennedy's embarrassing appearance at the Orange Bowl in Miami, when Roberto found himself in more trouble, this time in the United States. As a member of the 2506 Brigade who fought as a pilot flying sorties over the battlefield in Playa Giron in the Bay of Pigs, Roberto felt that Kennedy's visit was a slap in the face of the Cubans who yearned to return home. President Kennedy, having denied air cover for the Brigade in their last desperate hours of the Bay of Pigs fiasco, was now coming to Miami with Pepe San Roman, leader of the Brigade. At half time the ceremony included the handing of the Brigade flag to Kennedy and his promise to return the flag to a free Cuba. Knowing Kennedy's failure to order appropriate US air support that the Brigade desperately needed in order to establish a foothold on Cuban soil, Roberto was furious.

As a surviving member of the Brigade, Roberto requested an audience with the President, but his request was denied. He contacted several of his "friends" at the CIA to support him in his request for an audience with Kennedy to explain some of the facts regarding what actually happened and was happening in Cuba, and he was again rebuffed. For some reason, after all the work Roberto had done for the CIA they now thought of him as a "loose canon." On December 29, 1962, President Kennedy, after receiving the Brigade flag, promised to return it "someday" to a free Cuba. As of January 1, 2010 this day has yet to arrive and the Brigade flag remains on American soil, another presidential promise unfulfilled.

After the U.S. naval blockade of Cuba and the worldwide tension caused by the Cuban Missile Crisis of October 1962, President Kennedy made a promise to the Soviet Union that he kept: United States forces would not invade Cuba if the Soviets would remove all nuclear missiles from the island. Insodoing, Kennedy's promise perpetuated Fidel Castro's communist regime. Roberto Lance took Kennedy's pledge as an affront to Cuban expatriates living outside Cuba and those misfortunates who were forced to remain on the island and live under communist rule. Roberto made his opinion clear to CIA operatives in Miami, but the CIA was not interested in his "political incorrect" position on the Bay of Pigs debacle that Kennedy was trying to put behind. Any influence that Roberto may have previously wielded with his contacts within the CIA quickly evaporated, and his connections with the CIA were terminated.

After Roberto thought that he had seen the end of his relationship with the CIA, a further accusation of involvement in the assassination of President Kennedy surfaced. Fortunately for Roberto, nothing came of this; however, Roberto did get arrested twice for trying to smuggle weapons into Cuba to support the counter-revolution forces. He was caught each time; Miami was full of informants for the U.S. government, and many informants were Cuban security agents who, by then, had infiltrated Miami. Every move by any dissident in Miami was watched very carefully from Cuba. Roberto was threatened many times with arrest and jail, but because many Cuban-American politicians and ordinary Cubans in Miami considered him a real hero, the U.S. government did nothing but to keep a close watch on him.

This day-to-day intrigue put too much pressure on Roberto, and he suffered a minor breakdown. He realized that he had to back off from his emotional and personal involvement in high-stress, anti-Castro subversive activities and concentrate on his family and his own life. He tried different jobs, but his thoughts were always of his beloved Cuba. He went through very difficult emotional and economic times, and, although he was offered help from his closest friends who understood what he had done for a free Cuba, he rejected their support. Some of his closest friends thought that Roberto might need professional help for his depression but were afraid to broach this topic with him fearing it would alienate him even more.

With the fall of the Soviet Union and the liberation of Eastern European countries, Roberto hoped that the promise made by President Kennedy to the Russians about not invading Cuban soil was no longer valid since the Soviet Union as a world power no longer existed. Unfortunately, hopes, even based on actual historical data, may end up as merely empty hopes. To his great disappointment, Roberto realized that the US government was going to continue its economic sanctions of Cuba, and, other than nominal, cosmetic diplomatic petitions using human rights as an excuse, to do nothing regarding the political status. Cuba would remain communist; Roberto's hopes of someday returning to a free, democratic homeland were dashed.

Roberto was in a state of severe depression. Frustrated by the realization that he would never be able to set foot on Cuban soil again and heartbroken over the death of his beloved wife and two of his children in an automobile accident, Roberto' world was spiraling out of control. Roberto Lance, Cuba's first dissident, keeping true to promise he had made to himself to choose the day of his departure from this world, committed suicide with a bullet to his heart, believing that he would never be able to return to a free, democratic Cuba.

Roberto's funeral was attended by thousand of people who overflowed the small church of "La Hermita de la Caridad del Cobre," the Catholic Church of the Patron Saint of Cuba. His compatriots always considered him a true hero, a fighter for the independence of Cuba, as his grandfather had been before him during the Spanish American War. Instead of fighting Spain, Roberto had fought international communism. Those Brigadiers who had personally seen Roberto's aircraft trying to help them during the Bay of Pigs invasion surrounded his coffin, bedecked with the Cuban flag. Absent from the funeral were those unthankful, untrustworthy, unreliable CIA operatives for whom Roberto had risked his life so many times.

For many Cubans in the United States and elsewhere in the world who are buried outside their country of birth or nationality, it was far better to be interred abroad as free men and women rather than to be buried in a country controlled by a brutal, ruthless, totalitarian regime as in Castro's Cuba. Roberto was a victim of a revolutionary movement dedicated to communism and a way of life by which he could not live. And thus ended the life of Fidel Castro's onetime Chief of the Rebel Air Force, Roberto Lance, despondent at the end, but interred as a free man in a free country.

The Cigar Man

"The first farmer was the first man, and all historic nobility rests on possession and use of land

Ralph Waldo Emerson

José María Patrón was the owner of a small "vega" – a tobacco plantation – in the Cuban province of Pinar del Rio that is situated near the western tip of the Island. This area is globally recognized as having the richest soil in the world for the cultivation of tobacco leaves used for the manufacturing of the world famous "Cuban cigars." José María had inherited this land from his father Don Diego Patrón who had received it from the government as a reward for his heroic efforts in the War of Independence. A six feet, four inches tall and burly Black Cuban, Don Diego had fought on the side of General Antonio Maceo, another Black man and a national hero in the fight for Cuban independence.

The farmland was donated to Don Diego by the first president of the Republic of Cuba, but, unfortunately, Don Diego was required to wait two years before he could actually take ownership of the land. In those days, American authorities ruling Cuba after the Spanish American War did not believe that a Black man should be given access to such valuable land.

One of the many mistakes made by the Americans during their occupation of Cuba was to think of Cuban soldiers as part of a "rag tag" army, in spite of the fact that this army had defeated the Spanish Imperial Army in all ground battles. In reality, it was the desire of many American politicians to annex Cuba. Due to international knowledge made available by the press as to what had transpired in Cuba, this dream of annexation never materialized. From that moment on, the United States government exerted an almost paternalistic influence over Cuban politics. This influence became evident by the passing of the Platt Amendment, named after Connecticut Senator Orville H. Platt, which gave the United States the right to intervene in Cuban foreign and domestic affairs from 1901 up until 1934. One of the corollaries of this Amendment allowed Americans to purchase, at very small cost, some of the best sugar cane lands on the island. Fortunately at that time, Americans had little interest in the land reserved for tobacco cultivation.

Two other issues affected the Cuban-American relationship. One was pressure for Cuba to hand over territory in Guantanamo for the American government to establish a naval base. The second one was that the United States did not permit Cuban generals who fought against the Spanish Army for so many years before the San Juan Hill heroics to participate in the 1898 Treaty of Paris peace agreement. Had the Cubans not accept these two conditions, its independence would not have been granted.

Finally, on a bright, sunny morning at 9:00 AM, May 20, 1902, the American Stars and Stripes descended from the flag pole in the esplanade of the Palace of the Capitanes Generales in Havana, and the Cuban flag ascended, signaling the beginning of the Cuban Republic. Political authority was transferred from American General Leonard Wood to Don Tomás Estrada Palma, and it was President Estrada Palma who signed the land grants to the veterans of the Cuban War of Independence.

Doña María García, born in Spain, had been married to a man who owned land adjacent to Don Diego's property in the Pinar del Rio province, but was now a widow. They met at church, Don Diego Patrón went through the necessary of social rituals of courtship, and were married. On October 26, 1918, José María Patrón García was born. José María was born a "mulatto," meaning that he was a black male with "white" blood. His mixed blood was irrelevant in a Republican Cuba where white and Black men had fought side by side for their independence. Everyone born Cuban was considered first a Cuban, regardless of his or her race.

As José María grew up, he was taught how to plant and tend the tobacco plants on his father's farm that had doubled in size. The additional land belonged to his mother prior to her marrying Don Diego and was simply annexed to Don Diego's property. José María could hardly wait for his school vacations to help around the farm; he enjoyed planting tobacco and watching it grow to maturity. The soil was rich, the climate perfect, and the crop thrived. After finishing high school, José María decided to dedicate all his energy to running the tobacco plantation. His father appointed him manager of the entire property, which he oversaw for the next three years, until his father died of a short bout with pneumonia. He realized that he needed more technical education to be able to really compete and succeed on a higher level in the tobacco business and, with his father's permission, hired a loyal, capable replacement for himself. Content that the farm was in competent hands, José María registered at the University of Havana as a student in the College of Agriculture and Administration and began his studies in Agriscience and Technology.

While at the University he met a young law student named Fidel Castro Ruz. The friendship that developed between the two men was founded on Fidel's background on his father's farm in Oriente province and their mutual dislike of the dictatorship of President Fulgencio Batista who had come to power after the military coup on March 10, 1952. Perhaps influenced by the many stories told to him by his father about his own involvement in the War of Independence, José María decided to join the revolutionary group organized by Fidel Castro.

On July 26, 1953, Fidel Castro and 90 men including José María Patrón attacked the Moncada military barracks in the city of Santiago de Cuba in Oriente Province. José María sensed that the attack was going to fail, but he felt that blood would have to be shed in order to convince the Cuban people that they should oppose Batista's dictatorial government. During the battle, José saw his dear friend, Dr. Mario Muñoz, shot dead in front of him. He thought of Mario's lovely wife and daughter waiting for his return to their home in the city of Colón, and his heart broke. He asked himself, "Is all of this worth dying for?" That thought would remain with him for the rest of his life.

The attack on the Moncada Barracks was indeed a total failure; José María survived but was taken prisoner together with Fidel Castro, Castro's brother, and about a dozen other survivors of the attack. The prisoners were taken to Havana and, after a brief trial, were sentenced to prison at the Model Penitentiary on the Island of Pines just south of Cuba and later renamed in 1978 as the "Isla de la Juventud." Even though the rebels were sentenced to fifteen years in prison, on February 24, 1955, Batista signed an amnesty law enabling José María and the other members of the Moncada attack to go free. With hopes of bringing tranquility to the country after this attempt at a military coup, Batista's amnesty decree also included an increase in salary for all government employees. "Arturito's Law," as this sub-section of Batista's general amnesty document came to be known familiarly, was drafted by Cuban Senator Arturo Hernández Tellaheche.

After his release from prison, José María Patrón returned to his plantation in Pinar del Rio where he continued to enjoy his love for the soil and the cultivation of tobacco. He expected to be left alone to run his business, but this was not to be the case. The local police and the "Guardia Rural," the rural section of the Cuban army, expended an inordinate amount of effort to make his life miserable. Sometimes they would block the roads needed to move his tobacco leaves to the cigar factories, or they would simply confiscate the tobacco leaves and burn them. José had no recourse but to watch his harvest rot or be destroyed.

Meanwhile, Fidel Castro and the other participants in the Moncada attack left Cuba to suffer exile in Mexico. José María learned of their fate from the local newspaper and the radio news, and eventually concluded that he could not remain on his farm while Fidel and the others were away. He left his trusted foreman, now his manager, in charge of the plantation and flew to Mexico to join the others. After receiving brief military training from a Spanish ex-general of the Republican side of the Spanish Civil war, José María, Fidel Castro, his brother Raul, an Argentinean named Ernesto Guevara, and eighty-one other men, boarded the yacht "Gramma."

On December 2, 1956, they landed at "Las Coloradas" in Oriente Province, the most eastern province of Cuba. The landing was a disaster, and Batista's soldiers almost wiped them out to a man. Fortunately, a guide who knew the intricacies of the rough mountains guided the remaining men into the Sierra Maestra to escape from Batista's troops. José María felt that his current involvement with Fidel in these revolutionary actions were similar to his father's commitment in the original battles for the independence of Cuba. He also felt that he was involved in an honorable enterprise: to forcibly remove a dictator who was ruling Cuba by sheer military force.

José María became one of the early comandantes of the Cuban Revolution and fought bravely in several skirmishes against Batista's army, once receiving a minor wound to his left calf. However, at the mountain hideout in the Sierra Maestra where Fidel, Raul, and Ernesto "Che" Guevara had established their headquarters, José's wound became a "badge of honor." No other comandante suffered a wound while laying low at the Sierra

Maestra encampment. The other comandantes were too occupied talking to the foreign press or making plans for future attacks.

José María stayed at the Sierra Maestra until January 1, 1959, when news was received early that morning that President Fulgencio Batista and five of his generals had fled the island and gone into exile. There were two main reasons for Batista's defeat, one diplomatic, the other military. First, the United States government had withdrawn its monetary and political support, and, second, the rebels' January 1, 1958, victory at the Battle of Santa Clara which cut the island in two. Over the course of three days with a force of barely 300 men, "Che" Guevara was able to defeat a contingent of almost 3,500 of Batista's army that was also supported by ten armored tanks.

After their march towards the city of Havana and the consolidation of power by the rebels, José Maria was placed in charge of the department responsible for analyzing the agricultural needs of Cuba. This brought him in direct contact with "Che" Guevara who had been named Director of the Agrarian Reform (INRA) by Fidel. It did not take very long for the two men to dislike each other. José María, the older of the two, felt that "Che" was wrong in many of his policy decisions related to agriculture and was not afraid to say so to his face. José María knew how to run a farm, not only from the practical point of view but also from what he had learned at the University. He did not know that "Che" wanted to nationalize all the farms and create a Soviet-like agricultural reform. "Che" wanted the government to have absolute power over the Cuban agricultural system and, eventually, control over every facet of Cuban society. In other words, "Che" believed in creating cooperatives while José Maria believed in the value of small farms and free enterprise.

The final confrontation between the two men came when "Che" Guevara ordered José María to return to his tobacco plantation and nationalize it in the name of the "Revolutionary Government." José María refused and reminded "Che" that his property was earned by his father's heroism during the War of Independence. "Che" was so incensed by José María's outright refusal that "Che" used a demeaning and derogatory term to insult mulattos. José María remained cool and calm but responded that he had never dealt with people of color in his all white Argentina and reminded "Che" that he was now in Cuba where Black and white Cubans had always fought together for freedom. This refusal almost cost José María his life; luckily "Che" was not wearing his gun. What "Che" did was to order his bodyguards to immediately place José María under arrest and arrange for his transferal to the Cabaña Fortress where many executions had already taken place.

Fortunately for José Maria, Fidel was in an adjacent room when the confrontation occurred, heard the disturbance, and separated the two men who were just about to trade punches. Fidel convinced "Che" to rescind the arrest order. Fidel mentioned that José María Patrón had been a brave comandante who fought in the Sierra Maestra at the same time that "Che" was in the Escambray Mountains and at the Battle of Santa Clara.

Fidel said, "Wait until José María has time to acclimate himself to the new reality, and understand that we are going to do things differently from the past." This clearly meant that José Maria's tobacco plantation would not remain under his personal ownership since there is no such thing as personal ownership under communism except when the circumstances suit those in charge. When José María returned to his post in the Agricultural Department, a group of militia arrived in Pinar del Rio province and proceeded to nationalize all the plantations in the area, including José María's lands.

In view of his confrontation with "Che" and the executions of numerous friends at the Cabaña Fortress who had fought for the Revolution, José María concluded that he could no longer stay in Cuba and be part of the betrayal to the original principles of the Revolution: respect for human rights, freedom of the press, and free elections.

With great sorrow, José María contacted the Spanish Embassy in Havana. He knew that the militia was watching the Embassy, and, since he did not trust "Che," he took the precaution to assume a disguise as a member of the Embassy's cleaning staff. The fact that José María's mother had never become a Cuban citizen and retained her Spanish citizenship, as well as his past difficulties with the revolutionary authorities, helped expedite his petition for political asylum. Once he got past the guards outside the Embassy walls and entered the grounds he knew he could never leave the property. To do so would have meant certain death. That very same evening he was flown to Spain on a diplomatic plane. His landed at Madrid's Barajas International Airport on the day of his birthday, October 26, 1961, with only the clothes on his back and was given a few pesetas that were donated by members of the Embassy's staff.

While in Spain, José María worked as a gardener and a carpenter and managed to save enough money to plan his departure for Miami, Florida. Many of his friends from the Revolution had left the island in order to save their lives and established permanent residences in Miami. José María and those friends did not leave Cuba to establish new lives in the United States solely for economical reasons but in search of real freedom.

José María knew of the concept that "hard work is the road to success" as a tradition of the "American way," but asked himself, "What am I going to do?" His experience was in growing tobacco leaves and selling them to businesses that manufactured and distributed Cuban cigars. He had spent some time watching the workers rolling leaves, converting them into premium cigars, and had even tried to roll some cigars himself but was not good at it at all.

When he arrived in Miami from Spain he learned that thousands of other Cubans were also flying to Miami from Cuba on the "Freedom Flights" that were initiated during President Lyndon Johnson's Administration in the 1960's. Many of those newly arrived Cubans had been long-time cigar smokers and authentic "Cubans" were not available in the United States because of the embargo. The lack of a commodity that native Cuban men took for granted as part of Cuban social interaction and enjoyment created the opportunity José Maria need to begin his new business.

José Maria was working as a gardener and a carpenter to support himself, and managed to save $600 in a short period of time to use as seed money in a free lance cigar rolling manufacturing business. He carefully inspected and selected leaves grown in Puerto Rico, Brazil, and Virginia in order to make cigars that could compete with those manufactured in Cuba. He had to purchase leaves from many different areas in order to find plants that produced leaves with the texture, aroma, and depth of flavor equivalent to leaves that he had harvested back home in Pinar del Rio. José Maria hired two men who had many years experience rolling cigars back in Cuba who produced two hundred or so cigars each per day. José Maria personally visited the owners of local Cuban businesses, restaurants, grocery stores, and small bodegas with free samples of his new product to get them behind the counters. Initially, instead of packaging the cigars in fancy boxes, José Maria's were wrapped in plain cellophane paper.

His expertise in the evaluation of leaf quality gleaned from his early education on the plantation in Cuba was his ace in the hole; the cigars he sold were as good as the ones sold out of Cuba. These premium cigars were sold under the name of "Patrón." However, the fact that the quality of his cigars could compete with the legendary "Cubans" was not much to brag about. Many of Cuba's established tobacco entrepreneurs had gone into exile in Mexico, the Dominican Republic, Nicaragua, among others, and the quality of the tobacco being grown had deteriorated considerably under the communist government.

As his business prospered, José María heard of tobacco of superior quality that was being grown in Nicaragua. He flew to Nicaragua where he discovered tobacco plantations growing leaves that even surpassed the high quality of leaves he had grown back on his father's plantation. Taking advantage of the strong American dollar at the time, he was able to purchase land in Nicaragua and grow his own tobacco without a middleman. All the production was shipped to one of his two factories in Miami, rolled by additional experienced workers, and packed in elegant cedar boxes. José Maria was so proud of the quality of his American processed cigars that they were sold under the names of "Patrón 20" and "Patrón 1902," to commemorate the date when Cuba became independent from American and Spanish rule. Many other trademarks were to follow, all with meaningful dates added to his name. His cigars have been sold all over the world and have won many medals and awards as recognition given only to the very best cigars.

In 2002, while attending a convention of "Spectacular Cigars," he stayed at the Moscow Renaissance Hotel and visited the cigar boutique in the lobby. He found a wide variety of his own "Patrón" cigars for sale and experienced a flashback to his youth planting, tending, and harvesting his leaves in Cuba. A tear rolled down his cheek as he realized that now his cigars were well known all over the world except in his beloved country of Cuba.

José María Patrón, now ninety-one years old and in excellent health for a man of his age, spends his time in Nicaragua walking among the tobacco plants and in Miami supervising his many tobacco factories. He represents one of many success stories of Cuban expatriates who escaped the nightmare of a communist regime and became successful in the United States. By using his expertise in tobacco and applying his desire to provide for cigar aficionados a product of the highest quality, José Maria now enjoys the envy of the cigar producers back in Cuba who have been steadily losing market share trying to compete with a superior product. His friends in Miami Beach still affectionately refer to José Maria as "The Cigar Man."

The Confession

"Coercion. The unpardonable crime."

Dorothy Miller Richardson

General Sergei Alejandro Alejandrovich, the only Russian speaking member of the Cuban Revolutionary Army, was on his deathbed. Sergei had been a heavy smoker since his teens, and the cancer had finally caught up with him. His doctors had given him about a year from the time of the diagnosis, but the cancer had metastasized to his liver and brain shortening his lifespan to only three, at most four, months from the day the tumor appeared on his lung X-rays. The general, resting at home with a morphine patch on his back to allay the pain, summoned his only son, Lieutenant Colonel Jorge Alejandro, for what turned out to be their last conversation.

Sergei, the son of Russian immigrants who came to Cuba after the Russian Revolution, was born in the city of Colón in Matanzas Province on October 27, 1930. His father, Yuri Alejandro Alejandrovich, was a communist sympathizer and remained so until his death. He was born in the city of Orenburg, close to the Ural Mountains but in the European area of the Soviet Union. Yuri and his wife, Galina, left the Soviet Union for England in 1920 since many refugees were allowed to immigrate to the United Kingdom at that time. From there they traveled to Cuba and were welcomed by friends who had already established themselves in the city of Colón.

As a merchant in the city, nobody knew or cared about Yuri's political sentiments. During the years prior to Castro's rise to power, both elected and non-elected presidents tolerated the then small communist party. The children in the neighborhood came to Sergio's home every Sunday morning after Mass to read their favorite comic strips: "Superman" and "Flash Gordon." Ironically, these children were innocently enjoying the exploits of these superheroes in the newspaper "Hoy," which was also the mouthpiece of the Cuban communist party. Sergei, better known by his childhood friends as "Sergio," the Spanish equivalent, grew up as a healthy, competitive, and well-liked boy. Tall, dark haired, and lanky, he excelled in high school and upon graduation entered a military school in Havana. He quickly attained the rank of lieutenant and became the youngest officer to be sent to The School of the Americas in Panamá. One integral part of his preparation was to study intelligence work and develop techniques to identify potential political assassination plots and to prevent their success. He was only nineteen years old when he returned to Cuba from Panama, and was assigned by President Carlos Prio Socarras to work as an Intelligence Specialist with Colonel Martin Elena, commander of the Moncada Military camp in Santiago de Cuba in Oriente Province, the eastern-most province of Cuba.

Early in 1952, Lieutenant Sergio Alejandro was promoted to Captain and assigned as an aide to Colonel Martin Elena. He was elated with this promotion and was sure that the Army was the correct choice of profession. With little warning, on the early morning of March 10, 1952, the unimaginable occurred: General Fulgencio Batista overthrew the democratically elected President. Batista was convinced that he had no chance of winning the election fairly, and so he orchestrated a coup d'etat that sent Carlos Prio Socarras into exile in Mexico.

The Army at Columbia Headquarters supported Batista and bragged that they had taken power without bloodshed. They called the event, "The Blue, White and Brown" for the colors of the Police, Navy and Army uniforms. This usurpation of power by means of a military coup marked the beginning of many tragic events that followed during Batista's reign and continued beyond his expulsion from power by Fidel Castro and his rebels on January 1, 1959.

In the middle of the military events, Colonel Martin Elena, not a politician but a true democrat, refused to accept Batista's request to join his government, even though Batista promised to promote him to the ranks of general. After Martin Elena's refusal to align himself with the new dictator and Batista's carrot in the form of a promotion, he requested to be discharged from the Army. Batista granted his request, and he joined the civilian ranks. Martin Elena had a strong engineering background, and he was told that "Rayonera de Matanzas," a rayon manufacturer company in the city of Matanzas, was looking for an executive with a background in mechanical engineering. His credentials as a leader and his technical background fit the bill and he clinched the position of manager and CEO of "Rayonera de Matanzas."

Captain Sergio Alejandro, in sympathy with his friend and with great emotional pain, also chose to resign his commission. Sergio's father was not pleased about his son's decision because he had hopes that Batista would assign some veteran communists to his cabinet, as he had done on previous occasions, therefore enhancing Sergio's chances of quicker, more impressive promotions. Yuri was even more unhappy when his son accepted a position as Military Instructor at the Virginia Military Institute where some of his friends from The School of the Americas were working.

While teaching in Virginia, he received news of Fidel Castro's failed attack on the Moncada Army camp on July 26, 1953. This attack amounted to nothing, and Sergio did not attribute too much importance to this isolated exhibition of political dissension. However, he was very surprised that Fidel was not executed for his attempt to overthrow the government and only sentenced to fifteen years in prison at the Island of Pines Penitentiary. In any event, Sergio was sure that Fidel Castro's imprisonment would end this revolutionary episode in Cuban political history.

On February 24, 1955, General Fulgencio Batista won the Presidency of Cuba in a one-sided election. To prove to the people that he was serious about his promise for a peaceful Cuba, he proposed a general amnesty; Fidel Castro and the survivors of the Moncada attack were included in this gesture of amnesty. After their release from prison, the Castro brothers were shipped off into exile to Mexico. Batista was confident that with these two men out of the country there was one less problem for him to worry about.

Months passed. Sergio's family kept him informed of the events occurring in Havana; students at the University were angry that a democratic government had been supplanted with a miltary dictatorship. A number of students manifested their opposition to Batista and his regime with speeches, rallies, and demonstrations. Castro secretly return to Cuba from Mexico to restart the revolution from his military stronghold in the Sierra Maestra Mountains. Sergio's family encouraged Sergio to join Castro in the mountain camp believing that Fidel's mission was to reinstate a democracy. To distance himself from his followers with communist sympathies and, in so doing, to cloak his own communist leanings, Fidel sent known sympathizers and "card carrying" members of the Party out of the mountain hideout. Sergio's impressive military record, his early opposition to Batista, and the resignation of his army commission made Fidel welcome him when he arrived at the rebel camp.

After the successful revolution on January 1, 1959, and after Batista fled Cuba, Sergio's intelligence gathering and his analysis regarding the sentiments of the general public became invaluable to the new revolutionary government. From the moment he arrived at the Sierra Maestra to his retirement from the military many years later, the now "General" Sergio Alejandro, kept a very low profile. Even the chief of the Rebel Army, Raul Castro, had very little contact with him. General Sergio ran the Directorate General of Intelligence (DIG) and was responsible only to Fidel. As a result, Sergio's had virtual autonomy and his decisions were never discussed with or questioned by anybody other than Fidel.

In February 1960, the Soviet Union began its intervention in Cuba with the arrival of Anastas Mikoyan. Sergio was involved in obtaining one hundred million dollars in credit and the marketing of a million tons of sugar to the USSR for each of the next five years. He was the only one who could look the Soviet representatives directly into their eyes and communicate in their language. This was the beginning of Soviet Union predominance in the political, economic, and military life in Cuba. If one contribution made by General Sergio Alejandro Alejandrovich and his Directorate is to be singled out, it was his insertion of moles in the United States to infiltrate all levels of security departments, including the Pentagon, the CIA, the FBI, the NSA (National Security Agency), and the Department of State, among others. How could Sergio accomplish such widespread infiltration of the most sensitive departments of United States' security? The KGB and the Soviet Embassy in Washington, D.C., were his cohorts in this masterful plan of espionage. Sergio was also in charge of insertion teams placed in South Florida, especially in the area of Miami, where most counter-revolutionary groups had established their headquarters. Another of his responsibilities was to be in charge of the personal security of Fidel's life. In spite of several attempts on Fidel's life, none came even close to succeeding. This security plan created by Sergio consisted of five zones around Castro where high level surveillance and superior personal protection was critical. Sergio's "five rings of protection" were impenetrable.

Immediately prior to the execution of the invasion of the Bay of Pigs, "Bahia de Cochinos," General Sergio informed Fidel as to the exact time and place of the landing, what military equipment would be used, and the strength of the invading force. In spite of this advanced knowledge on the part of Fidel and his militia, the approximate 1,300 members of "Brigade 2506" made courageous advances on Cuban soil in Playa Girón, the area of the landing. But Castro's Air Force, using "Sea Fury" planes Batista had previously obtained from England were instrumental in rebuffing the attack, and the landing was thwarted. American-backed air support for the invaders never materialized; ninety exiles in the Brigade were killed and the rest were taken prisoner.

With the Soviet Union's deeper involvement in Cuba, General Sergio became the KGB's and the Russian Military Intelligence's (GRU) right hand man. Sergio approved operation, code-named "Anadyr," which established ballistic missiles and deployed Ilyushin II-28 attack aircraft in Cuba prior to the nuclear weapons that were to follow. In fact, General Sergio was in the Control Center on October 27, 1962, when Castro gave the order to launch a Soviet SA-2 surface-to-air missile to shoot down an American U-2 reconnaissance flight, piloted by Air Force Major Rudolph Anderson, which was flying over Cuban air space to photograph an SS-4 launching site in San Cristobal, Pinar del Rio. Major Anderson was killed, the only American combat fatality in the Cuban Missile Crisis.

The United States finally learned that its intelligence system had been compromised. As early as August 1962, KGB defectors Anatoly Golitsyn and Lieutenant General Ion Pacepa informed the CIA that a Signal Intelligence listening station had been built at Lourdes, south of Havana. In all the years that General Sergio had served Fidel Castro, he did not recall a more furious Fidel than when Nikita Khrushchev ordered the Soviet nuclear missiles removed from Cuban soil. Sergio tried to calm Fidel by reminding him of President Kennedy's promise not to invade or allow any other country to invade Cuba. He further tried to calm Fidel by mentioning that there will always be Soviet nuclear submarines in Cienfuegos Bay. Nothing that General Sergio said made the slightest change in Castro's anger. To demonstrate his hate for the United States and especially President Kennedy, Fidel called a meeting of his Directorate General of Intelligence (DGI), the Russian Military Intelligence (GRU) and, most importantly, the two heads of the KGB in Cuba, Aleksander Nikolayevich Shepelin and Vladimir Yefinovich Semichastny. The topic of discussion was the "elimination" of President Kennedy. The two KGB operatives pointed out that there were other parties that also desired JFK's "elimination." The CIA was unhappy with Kennedy's plan to end the war in Vietnam, and the Mossad, Israel's national intelligence agency, was indignant with Kennedy for opposing Prime Minister Ben Gurion's plan to develop an Israeli atomic bomb for self-defense. Ben Gurion himself felt that Kennedy's unyielding opposition over Israel's right to obtain nuclear weapons was an affront to Israelis and to the future security of the Israeli nation. Leaders in Belgium and other European countries also expressed their unhappiness with several of Kennedy's international policies.

Of all the years of support and loyal service to Fidel, this was the first time that General Sergio disagreed with the plan to murder the President of the United States. He repeated that Cuba had already managed to neutralize the United States with the promise given to Premier Nikita Khrushchev not to invade Cuba.

Fidel's answer to his argument was, "We have to strike while the iron is still hot; besides nobody will accuse us of the crime since we have no reason for it." As a result of Khrushchev's decision to accede to Kennedy's demand to remove Soviet missiles and launch sites from Cuba, the groundwork for the assassination of JFK was established.

From October 22, 1962, when Kennedy publicly addressed the nation on the Cuban Missile Crisis to the morning in Dallas, Texas, November 22, 1963 when he was assassinated on the street outside the Texas School Book Depository, a sophisticated plan was drawn up to accomplish the mission. A Bulgarian assassin on the KGB's payroll was supposed to kill the "patsy," Lee Harvey Oswald, after he shot Kennedy from the sixth floor corner window. This plan to eliminate Oswald after Kennedy was assassinated failed when Oswald was quickly arrested and taken into custody. Those in charge of the conspiracy were forced to go to their backup member of the plot, Jack Ruby, the perfect mole. The elimination of Oswald by Jack Ruby on the morning of November 24 at the Dallas Police headquarters sealed all of the potentially compromising contacts even though, in reality, Oswald was considered an expendable pawn. General Sergio never could get all the details of the plan, but he later learned that some of his CIA moles had been taken over by the KGB and worked out the logistics necessary to permanently silence Oswald immediately after Kennedy was killed.

When Lieutenant Colonel Jorge Alejandro, General Sergio's only son, knelt at his father's deathbed, he learned the long-hidden truth behind the assassination of President Kennedy. Sergio also told his son that nobody would ever believe what he had just been told. Even classified documents created during President Lyndon

Johnson's term of office and certainly those of the CIA would never see the light of day. What worked in favor of those who covered up this crime was the large number of foreign departments who, for one reason or another, hated the young President. In order to complicate the truth further, General Sergio concocted a plan of misdirection. He had operatives in Miami spread misinformation associating the blame of Kennedy's assassination on members of a powerful ultra-radical group from the exiled community of Cubans. The rumors spread by Sergio's agents accused this vigilante group of orchestrating the assassination in retaliation to Kennedy's promise to Khrushchev never to invade the island and unseat communist control. The only living person who could shed light on this issue is Fidel Castro and, perhaps, his brother Raul, but this definitely will never happen.

On his deathbed and with diminishing breath, General Sergei Alejandro Alejandrovich's last words to his son, Jorge Alejandro, were, "I'm sure that my soul will rot in Hell forever, but I cannot leave this world without having confessed my role in the plot to murder President John F. Kennedy, a truly unpardonable crime."

Celestino Heres, Ph.D., is a retired Professor of Computer Systems at the University of Connecticut at Stamford and at the Norwalk Community Technical College, Norwalk, CT. Born and raised in Cuba, Dr. Heres graduated from North Carolina State University in Raleigh. He has been an educator and Computer Systems consultant to Perkin-Elmer, Dun and Bradstreet and many other corporations. Dr.Heres is also the author of *The Reluctant Revolutionary* © 2003 that contains additional tales about the Cuban Revolution.

Richard Anderson, Ed.D., is a retired high school Teacher of English who worked with his friend "Tino" on the editing of *The Reluctant Revolutionary* © 2003 and helped in the editing and layout of this collection.